WHY VOTE LIBERAL DEMOCRAT 2015

WHY V**2015**TE LIBERAL DEMOCRAT

JEREMY BROWNE

Biteback Publishing

First published in Great Britain in 2014 by
Biteback Publishing Ltd
Westminster Tower
3 Albert Embankment
London SE1 7SP
Copyright © Jeremy Browne 2014

ISBN 978-1-84954-735-2

10 9 8 7 6 5 4 3 2 1

A CIP catalogue record for this book is available from the British Library.

Set in Chaparral Pro

Printed and bound in Great Britain by
CPI Group (UK) Ltd, Croydon CR0 4YY

To my dad, who died, prematurely, this year.
He was not party-political, but he imbued in
me a combination of liberal internationalism,
a patriotic and resolute British individualism,
a willingness to question received orthodoxies
and a commitment to public service.

Contents

Introduction: Britain in Crisis ix

Chapter 1   The Liberal Age 1

Chapter 2   Freedom 18

Chapter 3   Opportunity 34

Chapter 4   Decentralisation 49

Chapter 5   Sustainability 65

Chapter 6   Globalisation 82

Conclusion: A Liberal Party of Government 99

Acknowledgements 103

About the Author 105

Introduction:
Britain in Crisis

Thursday 6 May 2010, 10.00 p.m.

The polling stations have closed at the end of an epic, rollercoaster general election campaign. None of the three principal parties have seized a decisive advantage; none have fallen by the wayside either. Almost all outcomes remain possible. As the process of counting the ballot papers begins, the only certainty is that nothing is certain.

Britain is looking into an economic abyss. Our country has endured the worst recession for generations. Our economic prospects are bleak. Unemployment has risen and is widely predicted to get worse. The government is running an unsustainable budget deficit, clocking up an extra £430 million of debt every day. Across Europe, only Greece, being dragged helplessly into bankruptcy, is borrowing more as a proportion of their national income.

The economic panic elsewhere in Europe has not yet gripped Britain, but pessimism and anxiety are rife. Fears abound that we will struggle to deal with our burgeoning debt, forcing interest rates up to ruinous levels. The prospects for businesses and job creation appear desperate. The affordability of essential public services is in doubt. Expert criminologists, and some politicians, predict soaring rates of crime and the wider erosion of civic society.

Across the country, from town halls and municipal sports centres, the election results are filtering in. No clear picture is emerging.

Labour has suffered its second worst share of the vote since the introduction of universal suffrage, but is showing more resilience in its marginal held seats. The Liberal Democrat breakthrough has not materialised but nor has the party been substantially squeezed. The Conservatives are winning the most votes and the most seats, but are falling short in key battleground constituencies. As dawn breaks, political clarity remains elusive.

Friday 7 May 2010

Exhausted politicians and sleep deprived commentators are navigating the new and unfamiliar post-election landscape without an up-to-date map. It has been thirty-six years since Britain had an inconclusive general election result. A full-blown coalition, now under active consideration, has not been tried in Britain since the exceptional circumstances of the Second World War. Our economy needs decisive attention and our country requires resolute leadership. For those of an unsteady disposition, it is an unnerving time. Only an exceptional, bold, imaginative and magnanimous political solution will be an adequate response to the magnitude of our collective national predicament.

The case against the Liberal Democrats in 2010 took two main forms.

The first was a matter of credibility. This problem has inevitably dogged the Liberal Democrats as decades in the political wilderness erased any collective memory of the party holding office. Success at other levels of politics, most particularly in local government, went some way to addressing this deficiency, but only some way.

Britain was seen as having two governing options: Labour or the Conservatives. To opt for the Liberal Democrats was seen by many as essentially abstaining from the responsibility of choosing a national government. Thus a self-fulfilling prophecy was created: voters rejected the Liberal Democrats because the party could not reasonably be expected to be in government. It was a 'wasted vote'.

The credibility barrier also featured another dimension. Many who conceded that the Liberal Democrats could plausibly enter government, or were willing to vote for its candidates even without this expectation, entertained doubts as to whether the party really had the backbone to make big and tough decisions at the national level.

Damning the party with limited praise, voters would acknowledge the impressive track record of local Liberal Democrat councillors, before then asserting that these qualities would not translate to the national stage. The self-fulfilling prophecy was reinforced: the Liberal Democrats were deemed to not be cut out for national government but were denied the opportunity by their detractors to prove those very same detractors wrong.

These circumstances put the Liberal Democrats in an invidious position. All elections, rightly, involve politicians and journalists testing the strength of the different policy platforms. But the criticism of the Liberal Democrats has taken a different form. The party has been ridiculed for the naivety of its policies by politicians wearing the cloak of authority that government has bestowed upon them.

Thus, in 2010, Lord Mandelson, as part of a government that was presiding over a massive recession and a catastrophic budget deficit, still felt confident enough to belittle the Liberal Democrats, claiming, 'Their policies are a joke. They aren't serious. Their policies are almost unfathomable and certainly unaffordable.' A columnist writing in the *Daily Telegraph* in the immediate aftermath of the election also mined this seam, claiming of the Liberal Democrats that 'their plans deserve to be put in the box labelled "fantasy" and no more talked about in polite society'.

Alternatively, assertions have been made about the dangerous recklessness of Liberal Democrat policies, without the party having an opportunity to demonstrate in government that the accusations made by their detractors were groundless.

As an example of this full-on unsubstantiated charge, perhaps another columnist, also writing in the *Daily Telegraph* just days before the 2010 general election, provides a definitive illustration: 'Clegg is beyond doubt the most left-wing major UK politician in a generation.'

The second case against the Liberal Democrats in 2010 was more particular to that general election, and was made with increased shrillness and hysteria as polling day approached. It concerned the perceived dangers of a hung parliament.

This outcome, caused by no party being able to persuade the electorate of their suitability to govern alone, was routinely described as leading to a government that would inevitably be weak, unstable and discordant. It was conveniently overlooked that many majority single-party governments of recent decades, particularly those of John Major and Gordon Brown, could objectively be said to possess those traits in abundance. Coalition government was widely thought to be incapable of being sustained for a whole parliament. It was even said to be inherently 'un-British'.

Pillars of the status quo establishment lined up to give their authoritative thumbs down to a hung parliament with the possibility of coalition government. Peter Hargreaves of financial advisers Hargreaves Lansdown said: 'A hung parliament will be the worst possible result for our economy. It could trigger a similar situation to the 1970s, when the government was eventually forced to go to the International Monetary Fund for a loan.' Savills, an upmarket estate agency, said: 'The worst outcome for the housing market would be a hung parliament.'

David Frost, director general of the British Chambers of Commerce, said: 'Businesses are right to be wary about the prospect of a hung parliament.' General Sir Richard Dannatt, former Chief of the Defence Staff, warned against the election 'producing no clear answer', adding, 'We owe it to ... our servicemen and women to do better.'

The Centre for Business and Economic Research was extremely

confident in its predictions, claiming that a hung parliament could cost consumers as much as £5,000 a year, interest rates could rise seven-fold to 3.5 per cent, the pound could fall and financial markets could go into 'full-scale crisis'.

Many newspapers and media commentators shared this analysis. The *Daily Mail* said: 'Britain needs an outright winner in this election – not the disaster and uncertainty of a hung parliament.' The *Daily Telegraph* expressed anxiety that a coalition government 'could cut the value of pensions, push up mortgage rates and generally endanger recovery'. A historian writing for the *Daily Mail* provided a fuller context, writing under a headline on the eve of poll which read: 'Paralysed Britain: the last time we had a hung parliament … and the chilling parallels with today.'

Perhaps most extraordinary was a mock election broadcast, produced by the Conservatives, on behalf of the 'Hung Parliament Party'. The spoof party would, it was claimed, guarantee 'indecision and weak government', 'disastrous' hikes in interest rates and would 'paralyse' Britain. The broadcast also featured a picture of Gordon Brown standing in Downing Street with the message: 'This is what a hung parliament looks like.'

The supposed consequences of a hung parliament were thus presented to voters as having two features: an apocalyptic impact on the economy and the inevitability of a Labour–Liberal Democrat coalition with Gordon Brown remaining as Prime Minister. It was asserted without equivocation by many Conservatives during the 2010 general election campaign that the Liberal Democrats would automatically default to a coalition with Labour.

This supposed underlying preference was still being held up as the default option long after the general election polling day. Writing in the *Daily Mail* on 12 May 2010, one senior political commentator said:

> Now Clegg is entering into a conspiracy with Labour to steal from the British people their choice – and impose another unelected Prime Minister

in a backstairs stitch-up. 'Vote Clegg and get Brown' were the taunts in
the election run-up. Now it seems that mantra should have been 'Vote
Clegg and get Miliband'. Until Clegg's act of betrayal, there seemed every
chance that the Tories and the Lib Dems could get together ... now that
is out of the question.

In the same newspaper, on the following day, responding to the
formation of a Conservative–Liberal Democrat coalition, another
commentator, Max Hastings, was among the first of many observ-
ers to predict an early demise for the newly constituted government,
requiring another general election 'almost certainly within a year'.

2014: The coalition government enters the final year of its five-year agreement

There have been inevitable disagreements, although often within
parties as much as between them. The government has benefited
from a high degree of stability. Margaret Thatcher was driven from
office after a revolt by her own Chancellor and Deputy Prime Minister. John Major was forced to resign as leader of his party in an
ultimately unsuccessful attempt to flush out internal critics of his
premiership. Tony Blair, despite giving Labour an unparalleled
stretch in government, was forced from office by the allies of his
own Chancellor. Gordon Brown survived against a constant backdrop of conspiracy, plots and Cabinet-level resignations. The 2010
coalition government, by comparison, has been a model of calm
and harmony.

Most importantly, the deep economic darkness of 2010 has been
dispelled. More needs to be achieved, but the progress made is
beyond dispute. The budget deficit has been significantly reduced.
Interest rates have remained low for years, and when they are
increased it will be in response to economic success, not a panic
reaction to economic failure. More people are in work than ever

before, confounding predictions that unemployment would rise. Taxes have been cut for millions of people earning typical incomes. The economy is growing more strongly than in other comparable Western countries.

The Liberal Democrats have been on a remarkable journey. Britain has been on a remarkable journey.

Chapter 1

The Liberal Age

This book has one big contention: that we live in the liberal age, and that it would be perverse not to embrace the spirit of our time by electing a government suffused with liberalism.

Liberalism is the belief in freedom and, by extension, opportunity. The freedom to be who you are; the opportunity to be who you could be. It is the ideology of personal liberation from authoritarianism, suppression, coercion, conformity and ignorance.

The questions then are: 'Freedom from whom?'; 'Freedom for whom?'; and 'Freedom to do what?' – and it is worth examining each of these in turn.

At the heart of liberalism is the individual. Liberals start with the recognition that every person is born free; the task is to protect him or her from the excessive or arbitrary use of power and to guard the liberties of the individual against abuse from authority.

That is why protection against an over-mighty and presumptuous state is a core liberal objective. The state should be the servant of the citizen, not his or her master. The state should have no power over and above that which is granted to it by its people. It is not a natural entity: it has been formed by individuals to serve their interests.

Yet the world has long been full of states that rule over their people rather than serving them. In the worst cases, those in positions of authority actively suppress their own people. They imprison them without trial. They torture them. They restrict their freedom to express themselves. The state becomes more than an aggregate of the people; it becomes an entity in itself, with its own interests, in conflict with those of the people.

The most egregious examples of excessive state power are the most shocking, but all exercise of political power has the ability to exceed what is in the interests of those the state exists to serve. Even in more benign systems of government, vigilance remains necessary.

That is why liberalism is so concerned about the restriction of excessive and arbitrary power and the codification of government. It is why liberals favour transparency and accountability in government, a dispersal of power between the executive, the legislature and the judiciary, a free and vibrant media, and constitutionally enshrined rights and freedoms.

These systems are necessary to contain the state in a way that continues to serve the public interest. Liberals are not anti-government, but we are always wary of the potential of government to accumulate power, seeking to direct people rather than seeking instruction from them.

So, to the question 'Freedom from whom?', the first answer is 'the state'. But not all authority derives from the state. The individual citizen can also have his or her freedom restricted by other organisations. So liberals are concerned with restricting the power of the over-mighty, the distant and the unaccountable.

Big businesses can compromise the freedom of people. They can operate cartels or adopt monopolistic practices that curtail the free choices of consumers. They can maintain a working environment which threatens the safety of their employees or pay them exploitative wages.

Trade unions can help to prevent such abuses, but they can also compromise people's freedom themselves. They can restrict the right of an employee to go to work or seek to coerce a person into becoming a member against his or her wishes.

The media plays a crucial role in holding the powerful to account.

But it too can compromise individual liberty by using the power of mass communication to libel, slander or intrude upon the personal life of a private individual.

Even wider society can restrict the freedom of the individual. Anyone who does not conform to majority preferences can be discriminated against or ostracised.

Liberals, in all these cases, are champions of the underdog. Our cause is that of the violated and the defenceless. It helps to explain why the Liberal Democrats have never been heavily funded by either big businesses or trade unions: our loyalty has always been to the individual, not to any institution, group or vested interest.

To protect people from excessive and arbitrary uses of power, it can sometimes be necessary to galvanise the state in that cause. This is why liberals are not anti-government so much as anti-authoritarianism. The state can accrue too much power but, contained and scrutinised by the people, it can also protect the private citizen.

That is what prevents big businesses from deploying monopolistic practices or trade unions from operating 'closed shop' compulsory membership systems; it provides legal redress to a person who has been libelled by the media. The government can also protect the private citizen directly – from crime, for example – in a way that enhances, rather than detracts from, his or her freedom.

The full answer to the question 'Freedom from whom?' then, is 'the powerful'; people or organisations, including the state, that threaten the liberty of the individual.

To the question 'Freedom for whom?', the answer is 'the individual'.

The history of the last century was, in large part, about the struggle for freedom against the menace of fascism and communism – collectivist ideologies that placed the declared interests of the group above the rights and liberties of the individual. Socialism seeks to do the same, albeit in a more diluted form and on the basis of collective consent. The curtailment of freedom is acknowledged by the socialist, but dismissed as the price of greater equality.

Conservatism is more subtle. When it offends against individual liberty, it does so through a gentler form of social coercion, with the individual pressured into relegating his or her preferences behind those of the institution or the social class, whose behaviours and beliefs are reinforced by tradition, custom or collective prejudice.

The liberal belief in the primacy of the individual means the Liberal Democrats can never be a party that represents a particular social class, ethnicity or religion. Liberals do not believe that an individual's affiliation with a collective group is what defines them.

That does not imply that liberalism is entirely individualistic. People find an important sense of belonging and purpose through their memberships of groups, be they religious, sporting, social, charitable or commercial. Few people prefer isolation to inclusion, but our associations should be a product of choice, an expression of freewill. They should not be a label that is pinned on the individual.

And to the question 'Freedom to do what?', the answer is 'live your life as you see fit'. Liberals believe that free people, unconstrained by authoritarianism or collectivism, should make their own decisions.

Liberals favour free choice. Freedom to choose where you live, who you marry, what religion (if any) you practise. Freedom to start a business, expand it and keep a reasonable share of the product of your labour. Freedom to give your custom and to withdraw it. A suffocating 'one-size-fits-all' uniformity is the antithesis of liberalism.

Liberals are suspicious of groupthink and received orthodoxy, not because they are necessarily always wrong but because they are not necessarily right and always benefit from being challenged. Liberals shrink from conformity, whether formal or informal, which moulds the individual into a shape which satisfies the collective. Liberals stand against social pressure and the tyranny of the majority.

When liberals support state intervention, it is because it will either protect individuals from harm or enable them to expand their freedoms by increasing their opportunities: providing the education that liberates them intellectually; providing the transport infrastructure that liberates them physically; providing the free market systems that liberate them economically. Liberal freedom and opportunity is how every person can realise his or her full potential.

It is an outward-looking, forward-thinking, internationalist ideology – an enlightened belief that people who make free decisions are best placed to push forward the frontiers of knowledge and progress. Liberalism does not divide people into groupings that are defined by their antipathy towards, or fear of, other groupings. Instead, it sets them free to explore: new innovations, new alliances, new experiences; free trade, free people, free thinking.

Other ideologies start with the assumption that somebody else knows best – our predecessors in the case of conservatism; the all-knowing central planner in the case of socialism. Other ideologies are always concerned with outcomes – competing visions of the 'good society'. Liberalism, by contrast, is about processes – the intrinsic value of choice and free will to human welfare.

So where the other parties seek to direct people down the path of their choosing, the Liberal Democrats offer something else: the freedom to be who you are; the opportunity to be who you could be. We want people to be the authors of their own life stories, free to chart their own course, to go their own way.

The changes in Britain over my lifetime have been remarkable.

I was born at a watershed moment in the social development of our country. In 1970, Britain was coming out of a decade of dramatic liberal change. I cannot be the only person of my age who feels a twinge of envy at having missed out on such a period. The class fall-out of the Profumo Affair, the sexual fallout of the *Lady Chatterley's Lover* trial, the legalisation of homosexuality, the reduction of the voting age, the abolition of the death penalty, the invention of the contraceptive pill – all intermingled with Swinging London, Woodstock and England winning the 1966 World Cup.

Yet, looking back now, Britain was still mainly a conservative country during my childhood in the '70s. The colourful images that have come to symbolise the cultural liberation of the previous decade were made more vivid by the drabness of the backdrop. Not many British people had been at Woodstock, many had not even been to Swinging London, and the World Cup victory was watched on black-and-white televisions at home. Away from Carnaby Street and the heart of the Mersey scene, life for millions of people carried on much as it had before.

The Second World War only finished twenty-five years before I was born. Memories of rationing were still fresh. Popular culture in the '70s was heavily influenced by the achievements of my grandparents' generation – *Dad's Army*; *It Ain't Half Hot Mum* – who, now in their fifties, were the people running the country. The influx of immigrants from the Caribbean, East Africa and the Indian subcontinent was recent and acknowledged with clumsy, sometimes malicious, attempts at humour. In many parts of the country, a non-white face could still cause heads to turn. No non-white person had ever played football for England when I was a small boy.

Society, despite the upheaval of the '60s, was still very conventionally structured. For every bohemian rock star or artist, there were thousands of families where the husband worked and the wife looked after the children. The objective, whether it was a middle-class job as an accountant or a working-class job in a factory, was to find a job for life. Working hours were rigid. Shops opened only during these working hours, reflecting the division between the 'breadwinner' and the spouse at home who bought the bread.

The role of women was limited. Until 1975 a woman could be denied a mortgage unless it was underwritten by a man (typically her husband or her father). Those who worked mainly did so in a small number of 'female' professions. Our politics and businesses were run almost exclusively by men. There were far fewer female role models. It is amazing that Britain elected a woman Prime Minister in 1979; it was so far ahead of its time that it has not been repeated since.

Society was also very paternalistic and conservative. Everybody appeared to know their place in what was still a highly class-based country. Professional people worked in the same professions as their fathers; skilled manual labours worked in the same factories as their fathers. The state reinforced this rather undynamic and uniform order, providing not just healthcare and schools, but airlines, telephones, cars and even furniture removal. There was a heavy social conformity that was seen as providing a collective national glue, and did so, to an extent, but was also rather stifling.

It has been fashionable for many years now to look down on '70s Britain, with its orange sofas, brown and beige clothes and washed-out colour television pictures of industrial decline and disputes. It was sometimes pretty bleak but it was a necessary decade in our national journey, and for most children a reasonable time in which to grow up. I can remember taking the rubbish to the municipal tip with my dad during the Winter of Discontent, but not as vividly as I can remember watching Alan Sunderland score the winning goal in the FA Cup Final with him a few months later.

So although the '60s was a socially radical decade, it only represented the initial stages of a national journey towards liberalism. Pockets of society had become more liberal; the arts were more satirical and subversive, the media more challenging. But society as a whole was not in that place, or even close to it. Britain had yet to properly enter the liberal age.

The Britain of my childhood now feels pretty distant, another country where they did things differently.

The greatest difference today may be in the role of women and girls. Their high – and still rising – levels of educational attainment; their growing employment and earnings; their contribution to – and, increasingly, their leadership of – a range of organisations and institutions; their expectations and ambitions, and the expectations and ambitions others have for them. The changes are staggering.

It is true that the march towards full equality is not complete, and that the visibility of women in some aspects of society remains below that of men. There are 147 women MPs, 23 per cent of the total. Only four of the FTSE 100 chief executives are women. Even in professions dominated by women such as primary school teaching, a disproportionately large number of the head teachers are men.

Nonetheless, the trend is clear. Anybody looking forward forty years from my childhood would be amazed by how much progress women and girls have made, not how little. Social and cultural changes take decades to work fully through the system. By many indicators, women and girls are now succeeding in greater numbers than men and boys.

In 1970 just 32 per cent of new university students were women; by 2012 it was 58 per cent. Women under the age of forty who work full-time are, on average, now paid almost exactly the same as men. It is a mark of how far women have come that one of the biggest social concerns today is a lost cohort of disengaged, underachieving young men.

Most importantly, the outlook of younger women today is much less constrained by a sense of what is achievable or appropriate. They owe a debt to the women and men before them who campaigned for equality of opportunity, but they increasingly look beyond that legacy. The default assumption of most younger women is that they can reach their goals and succeed.

The differences today in attitudes towards race, homosexuality and disability are also pronounced.

In 1983, in the British Social Attitudes Survey, 20 per cent of white people said that they would prefer not to have a black person as their boss. By 2006 (from which point the question was discontinued), this figure had fallen to 9 per cent.

Again the march of progress remains uncompleted, and in many areas of national life people from ethnic minorities remain woefully under-represented; but again, a substantial distance has been travelled, and attitudinal shifts take time to work through the system. An Asian MP, Sajid Javid, being promoted to the Cabinet in 2014 is regarded by most as being healthily insignificant. Black football managers remain a rarity, but the England team has included so many black players it no longer even gets discussed.

When I was born homosexuality had only recently been legalised, yet it remained hidden, with many gay people fearful of the consequences of coming out. No gay MP, for example, felt able until the '80s to reveal his sexuality. Illiberal social attitudes persist, but again, it is striking how marginal those attitudes are now, and how rarely they are held by younger people.

The endorsement by parliament of gay marriage, by a large majority of votes, was the formal confirmation that homosexual relationships had progressed through all the stages of public opinion: abhorrence, disapproval, tolerance, genuine acceptance and, finally, benign indifference.

The everyday practical difficulties and discrimination experienced by people with disabilities remain very real, but this truth is not diminished by recognising the substantial progress that has been made in transforming public attitudes. The language used to describe people with disabilities has been totally overhauled. Practical progress, such as access for wheelchair users to public buildings and public transport, has been significant. The symbolic power of a massive stadium of paying customers watching the London 2012 Paralympics should not be underestimated.

These examples of substantial progress towards equality – for women, ethnic minorities, gay and disabled people – are the obvious manifestations of our increasingly liberal society.

Interesting, in a different way, is the parallel transformation in the customs and behaviours that bind us together. The changes, while barely noticeable in isolation, add up to a modern society that feels different from the past.

We are much more informal today, less buttoned up, less

deferential, less reserved. When I was a boy it would have been unthinkable for the presenters of *Match of the Day* not to wear a tie; now it would be curious if they did. The Prime Minister and others in senior positions of authority seemed to be more distant figures in my childhood, and would not have invited people to address them by their first names. We are much more comfortable about expressing emotion in public, including grief, in a way that would have been regarded previously as unseemly.

Sometimes this more relaxed style jars and the gravity of momentous occasions can be diminished. We remain in limbo with some aspects of social etiquette, uncertain whether holding open a door is a sign of good manners or could be regarded as a patronising hangover from a bygone era. But overall, in a way that is highly compatible with a more open, liberal, less conformist and stuffy society, we have adapted smoothly to significant social change. We are less censorious, more accepting of difference and slower to judge.

Globalisation has made us more cosmopolitan in our tastes and preferences. British cuisine, once an international joke, has benefitted from an infusion of diverse influences. The free market has brought to millions of people products, from avocados to hummus, that were regarded as prohibitively expensive or suspiciously exotic in my childhood.

Our entertainment options have proliferated. How strange it must be for teenagers today to imagine the excitement I experienced at their age when a fourth television channel became available. It was hard to think how we would cope with the bewildering degree of extra choice. The new channel also broke new boundaries, carrying alternative comedy, youth-focused programming and sports, like American Football, that were regarded as extraordinarily alien before the advent of satellite television and the internet.

And we are still in the foothills of the communications revolution. The generation that grew up with the internet is only now entering the workforce in significant numbers. When I was a child, people browsed through catalogues looking for a limited number of holiday destinations; now millions of alternatives are instantly available to them. The monochrome, one-size-fits-all marketplace of the past has been blown away. Instead, a dizzying array of choices is available to everyone.

Institutions have also adapted to keep pace with the times. Single-sex education is increasingly seen as anachronistic. Big companies have dress-down days. The Church of England has women vicars. The hierarchical and patriarchal society of my youth has become more democratic, more dynamic, more meritocratic and more fluid. It has become more liberal.

Perhaps nothing illustrates this change as starkly as the archetypal British pub. When I was a child I was not allowed in the pub. They were places for adults, mainly men, to drink alcohol and smoke cigarettes. If there was entertainment, it was darts; if there was food, it was peanuts.

But pubs are businesses and they adapt to changing tastes. There are still a few old-style 'boozers', but they are fewer and further between. Now children and families are widely welcomed. The selection of drinks has improved in both quality and quantity. More relaxed opening hours mean people can linger on a week-end afternoon. The food is rarely inedible and often delicious. The entertainment now includes quiz nights, televised sporting fixtures, musical performances, even art exhibitions.

The British pub holds a mirror up to British society – more relaxed, more female, more family-oriented, more customer-focused, more diverse, more welcoming and more liberal.

Economic liberal change has also made Britain a more vibrant, varied and dynamic country.

The economy of my childhood was inflexible, unresponsive and chronically weakened by industrial strife – the so-called 'British disease'. It was the era of loss, making nationalised industries, the 'closed shop', the 'flying picket', 'work to rule' and the three-day week.

It was unsustainable but it was also remarkably illiberal. Corporatism – the dominant creed of the day – sought to manage the economy by balancing the needs of the three key interest groups: business, labour and the state. Disputes were resolved in smoke-filled rooms or, if they were not, spilled out onto the picket lines. Competitiveness, productivity, customer satisfaction, value for taxpayers – all were relegated behind the maintenance of industrial politics. Meanwhile, new start-ups, self-employment, innovation and entrepreneurialism were all suffocated.

Just look, by contrast, at the energy and sheer diversity of our economy today.

The number of registered businesses has doubled in the past forty years from one million to two million, with many more micro-businesses also being created in addition to this figure. Instead of the marketplace being supplied by small numbers of lumbering giants, consumers are now served by an energetic, teaming host of new companies with new ideas.

The number of self-employed people has risen by 650,000 since just 2008. The proportion of the workforce that is self-employed is now 15 per cent, the highest level ever. Many of these people will succeed with their ambitions for their business, although some will not. But they will all experience the exhilaration and sense of liberation that comes from working for yourself, on your own terms, with your own business model and your own vision. They are being directly rewarded with the fruits of their own labour.

This major shift in our labour market is having a transformational impact on our overall economy. It has made us more nimble and flexible, better able to respond to new preferences and shifting demands. It will give Britain a competitive edge in a fast-changing global economy, where our greatest national asset is our ability to innovate and adapt.

The labour market is evolving to follow the contours of our changing society. More women are in work in Britain than ever before.

Some work part-time, usually by choice. The stark dilemma facing previous generations of women – motherhood or a career – can often now be avoided by balancing the two.

Many more people work from home, at least for some of the week. Major employers are also adapting, becoming more flexible around childcare requirements, more sympathetic to job-shares.

Methods of ownership are changing. More people have shares. Employee ownership is a feature of businesses ranging from the John Lewis Partnership to Royal Mail.

And in today's economy the customer is king. Where previously uniform products and inefficient services were provided by monopolistic monoliths, we now have thriving markets that both stimulate and respond to technological and lifestyle changes. Where once the state would, after an extended delay, install a home landline phone, now any number of providers will sell us any number of mobile devices. Where once we received three analogue television channels, we can now watch hundreds of digital channels, via satellite or cable, live or on demand at the time of our choosing. Where once we could only shop during working hours, we can now shop, in-store or online, whenever we wish.

None of this activity is planned or directed by politicians, bureaucrats, union barons or industry bosses. It is not being done by central planners who believe they know better than we do what is in our own interest. It is organic, fluid and unpredictable. It is open-sourced and crowd-sourced. It is decentralised and democratic. It is grass-roots-up, vital, unpredictable and fast-paced. Millions of people are reshaping our national economic and social landscape. This is, in all its glory, the liberal age.

Alongside these social and economic changes, we have also witnessed a profound change in political attitudes. Young adults today have vastly different expectations of the state, and of each other, than their parents' and grandparents' generations.

All age groups in Britain have become more socially and economically liberal over recent decades, but this shift is most pronounced among younger people.

It is not surprising that young people are most relaxed about socially liberal changes like gay marriage. The majority struggle to see what the fuss is about. But more counter-intuitive is that 18- to 24- year-olds are the most hawkish about the need for deficit reduction (despite shouldering a disproportionate burden of it). People born since 1979 – the so-called 'Generation Y' – are the greatest enthusiasts for low taxes, limited welfare and the exercising of personal responsibility. More than two-thirds of people born before 1939 regard the welfare state as 'one of Britain's proudest achievements'; less than one-third of people born after 1979 agree.

This scepticism about the paternalistic state extends to other attitudes held by younger people. They are less likely than previous generations to smoke, but more resistant to 'nanny state' tobacco warnings and restrictions. They are less antipathetic to big private sector companies, regarding their success as a result of freely exercised consumer choices. Younger people today are less collectivist, more free-thinking. They feel more smothered than protected by the comfort blanket of the big state social contract. They are more enthusiastic about starting their own company, working abroad or switching employers. They want to determine their own destiny.

The crucial insight is that, for increasing numbers of people in Britain today, personal liberalism and economic liberalism are no longer de-coupled. It is often said, by a commentariat constrained by the traditional orthodoxies of two-party politics, that the left have won the social arguments in Britain and the right have won the economic arguments. A 1–1 draw is declared after two generations of political tussle. I reject that analysis: I believe that liberalism has won both the social and the economic arguments. The true result is 2–0.

Britain is a liberal country, socially and economically. It is hard now to divide society between people who believe in free love and those who believe in free markets. Increasingly, people demand and expect to determine their own way of life, at work and at home, in their public and their private lives.

So emphatic has been the social liberal transformation of Britain that two great dangers liberals face today are cultural triumphalism and cultural relativism.

How we treat those who are discomforted by the liberal age, and by the pace at which its social norms have been established, matters deeply. After all, liberals should always recoil from groupthink and intellectual conformity. There is no place for the 'thought police' in a liberal society – self-appointed adjudicators of whether someone's beliefs are deemed acceptable to the sensibilities of the crowd. The law exists to enshrine our rights and freedoms and to prohibit behaviour that tramples on them; it does not need to be buttressed by a heavy-handed social standardisation. Coercive liberalism, advanced by many on the metropolitan left, is the antithesis of the free-thinking liberal individualism that has captured the mood of our time.

Liberals need also to avoid an alternative danger: the relativist view that liberal rights and freedoms are only suitable for some people and that their application, in some communities, would amount to gross cultural insensitivity, if not cultural imperialism. This is a dangerous nonsense. The law is the law and should apply to everyone. Just as liberals should be wary of buttressing the law with more subtle forms of coercion, so they should be wary of applying it selectively or partially when it conflicts with religious or cultural customs and practices. The freedom enjoyed by increasing numbers of people, both in their personal choices and in their economic opportunities, should be enjoyed by all, regardless of ethnicity or religion. Modern liberals should wear their liberalism lightly but retain a clear devotion to its universal and fearless application.

There will be some who accept that we do indeed live in a liberal age, but will argue that most of the changes that brought us to this point had little to do with politicians and, of those that did, many were introduced during periods of Conservative or Labour majority government.

This is true, but it overlooks the fact that the Liberal Democrats, and before that the old Liberal Party, have been the only consistent champions of liberalism throughout the period.

Only *some* members of the other parties have been committed to *some* aspects of liberalism, and only for *some* of the time. Many members of the Labour Party supported the expansion of personal freedoms that many members of the Conservative Party fought so hard to resist, while many members of the Conservative Party supported the expansion of economic freedoms that many Labour politicians fought hard to resist.

Neither offers a natural home to liberal reformers. Labour is, at heart, a collectivist party that places a greater emphasis on equality and solidarity than on liberty. The Conservatives, meanwhile, are primarily concerned with preserving the past and resisting change. As liberal Britain has taken shape, the Conservative Party has gone through a familiar sequence of reactions: outright hostility, predictions of impending doom, sullen acquiescence and, in time, accommodation. Conservatism is the post-rationalisation of changes made by others – hardly an ideology at all.

By contrast, the Liberal Democrats have been consistent and whole-hearted champions of the liberal cause. We have voted for necessary legislative changes in parliament, sometimes in a defiant minority, sometimes, when the tide of history sweeps others in behind us, as part of a victorious majority.

Crucially, we also stood for liberalism when the class-based social settlement of the post-war years tempted Labour and the Conservatives to settle on a mutually beneficial mush of quasi-socialism and corporatism. For decades, to be a Liberal Democrat advocating liberalism was to be consciously unfashionable, frozen out of the political club, inviting ridicule. How much easier it would have been for liberals to bow to the conformity of the time and dilute their beliefs.

By refusing the bend, however, we Liberal Democrats are now perfectly positioned to claim a valuable political inheritance. For liberal attitudes are not only dominant, they have matured. Gone are the days when liberalism was associated with a bohemian minority. Freedom of choice is now regarded as normal and unexceptional, but it is allied to an appreciation of the need to balance personal freedom with personal responsibility; an adult liberalism has emerged from its teenage rebellion.

Britain has, in the forty-four years since I was born, become a truly liberal nation. The issue for Liberal Democrats today is not whether enough people believe in liberalism. Not only do millions of people believe in it, they are busy living it, scratching their heads in bewilderment at the illiberal spasms to which our political class is still prone. No, the issue for the Liberal Democrats today is whether enough people who believe in liberalism are inclined to support the Liberal Democrats.

Far-sighted Conservative and Labour politicians know they are sitting on intellectual islands that are crumbling into the sea. To prevent further erosion, they hope to fortify their position by appropriating liberal themes.

But the question for voters in 2015 is this: when you seek a party in tune with the liberal age and your own liberal instincts, why choose those who are learning to hum along, when you could support those who wrote the song?

Chapter 2

Freedom

Personal freedom is the core proposition of the Liberal Democrats. Our contention is that every person should be at liberty to shape his or her own life. It is a simple, but powerful, idea.

It has intrinsic merit. Personal freedom is a virtue in itself; it is an end as well as a means to an end.

But personal freedom also has the merit of being the key to British success in the new globalised economy. Different countries have different advantages: Saudi Arabia, its oil; China, its vast population; Panama, its geographic location. Britain's advantage is the ingenuity and creativity of our people; qualities that depend on, and feed off, freedom.

The task is to liberate our people to achieve their potential, and thereby allow Britain to achieve its potential. Our country will never lead the world by being the most hierarchically ordered society, or by being the most egalitarian. Rather, our success relies on us being the most inquisitive, mobile and dynamic society – a place of invention, experimentation and thought leadership.

The Liberal Democrat belief in personal freedom makes us uniquely qualified to understand both this objective and the means by which it will be achieved.

The starting point for the Liberal Democrats is that people should be free to make their own choices unless, by doing so, they cause such harm to others that there is an overall net loss of freedom.

Disapproving of someone's behaviour is not a basis for restricting their freedom. Nor is a failure to share their preferences. Moral or religious codes provide a framework for many people's lives but they do not provide a justification for restricting the freedom of others unless codified in law.

People should be free to do what is foolish as well as what is wise. They should be free to act in ways which others may regard as harmful to their self-interest. The size of the majority wishing to restrict a person's freedom, or the fervour of their illiberalism, is not a basis for them to be able to subjugate the free choices of the individual.

To many people the principle of personal freedom will seem uncontroversial, but it is harder to uphold in practice. Members of the public can be quick to defend their own freedoms but then just as quick to seek to restrict those of others. The point at which liberals must be most vigilant in defending personal freedom is often when there is the greatest clamour to do the opposite.

Liberal Democrats, both outside and within government, have been the biggest exponents of personal freedom. We have championed the changes that have transformed our society. Legislation has, for example, recently been passed legalising gay marriage. Many people strongly opposed the change on the basis of their moral beliefs. I supported it, based on my liberalism.

People who are opposed to gay marriage are entitled to their view, but the solution for them is simple: do not marry a person of the same sex. Their objections to other people's choices are not a reason for restricting those choices in the absence of any demonstrable harm being done.

This liberal principle – that we should be free to do as we wish so long as we do not cause significant harm to others – is in danger of being eroded by a gradual widening of the definition of 'harm'. A new paternalism, motivated by a desire to reduce risk, improve public health and increase social welfare, is being promoted on the utilitarian basis of benefitting the majority. Despite the good intentions, this trend is pernicious, and should alarm all liberals.

Of course there are some freedoms that fail the harm test. Driving a car at excessive speed is prohibited because of the increased risk to pedestrians and other motorists. Anyone is free to listen to music, but not at excessive volume in the middle of the night if it disturbs their neighbours.

The same cannot, however, be said of most restrictions that many of our politicians now support. Branded cigarette packaging, sugar-coated breakfast cereals, high-salt fast foods, low-cost alcohol, online betting advertisements – all are now targets for politicians and pressure groups who think they are better placed than we are to protect our health or defend our morals.

With the Liberal Democrats, voters can choose a party that is committed not just to defending freedom, but to extending it too.

The debate is intensifying about how we treat people who are gravely ill and infirm at the end of their lives. There is no liberal basis for people of right mind to be prevented from dying in the way that they wish at a time of their choosing. It is presumptuous for the state to deem itself better equipped to make this decision than the individual concerned.

The notion of 'assisted dying', like equal marriage, is disconcerting for many people with strong religious convictions. But, as with equal marriage, they are free to live their own lives and, in this case, plan their own deaths, according to their own moral code. They should not force terminally ill people in considerable pain to endure the same level of suffering that they claim they would, in the same circumstances, bear themselves.

Once again, the harm principle needs to be sensibly applied: safeguards would be required to protect the mentally incapacitated or those who, in the absence of pressure from others, would not otherwise choose to end their lives. Assuming that such safeguards were in place, I would view 'assisted dying' as a humane and liberating measure.

The issue in a liberal society is not whether everyone approves of gay marriage or 'assisted dying', or whether we could reduce the risk of ill health by banning fatty foods and cheap alcohol. The issue is whether these freedoms, if exercised, would result in such a significant degree of harm being done to others as to justify their prohibition.

The Liberal Democrats, as a party committed to personal freedom above all, can be relied upon to set a high bar for any such test. Our instinct is to allow every person the freedom to make his or her own decisions.

A key part of what gives freedom real meaning is the ability for an individual to shape his or her own life. This goes beyond the right to make lifestyle choices without undue interference. It is about whether every person can determine their destiny or is obliged instead to be swept along by the collective current.

Liberal Democrats exist to give people this freedom. It informs all of our thinking.

On pensions: retired people who had paid into savings schemes were previously obliged to buy an annuity. This system existed under both Labour and Conservative governments. Now the Liberal Democrats have given retired people the freedom to decide how they spend their own money. Some might use part of their savings to help a grandchild with a deposit for a new flat. That is their decision; previously it was not allowed. Labour's response to the Liberal Democrats extending this freedom was to assert that pensioners could not be trusted to spend their own money.

On welfare and work: poorer people under Labour became more reliant on the state. They paid more tax on their earnings and in return received more benefits. The combination of lost earnings and increased state largess meant many people made a rational decision to not work and be dependent. The Liberal Democrats have reversed that presumption, cutting taxes for people on low incomes to ensure it always pays to work. The result is greater self-reliance and independence.

On public services: the traditional model has been top-down, with the service provided at the convenience of the state and with the individual expected to keep quiet and be grateful. We are turning this model on its head, ensuring that the system is designed to respond to the needs and preferences of service users. Where you go to school, how you die or give birth, to which doctor or hospital you entrust your care – in a liberal society, these decisions should be taken by people, not bureaucrats.

On crime: here we start by recognising the need to protect people from those who threaten their most basic freedoms. Anyone who is too afraid to venture out of their home at night is not free. Even if they have not been a victim of crime, their fear has turned their property into a prison. So the combatting of crime and the creation of a safe society is a crucial component of liberalism.

The Liberal Democrats in government have overseen a fall in crime. It is now at its lowest level in England and Wales since the independent survey began in 1981. The chance of being a victim of crime today is about half what it was twenty years ago. There have been even more dramatic falls in categories of acquisitive crime like car theft, but the falls for the most serious crimes, including murder, have all been sizeable.

There are many factors that contribute to falls in crime. More sophisticated methods of investigation such as DNA testing have had a powerful deterrent effect, as have the technological advances that make cars and possessions harder to steal and houses harder to enter. But policy, too, has had an effect, with a greater emphasis on community crime prevention and offender rehabilitation. While not all of this is down to the Liberal Democrats, it is still noteworthy that, despite being derided by our opponents for being 'soft on crime', we have presided over lower crime levels than when either of the other parties governed alone.

The corollary of freedom is responsibility: the two go hand-in-hand, each relying on the other for its true meaning and full value. That is why the two cannot, in any mature discussion of liberty, be separated. After all, the ability to exercise freedom responsibly is what distinguishes adults from children. It is also what separates free men and women from prisoners.

That is clear-cut and understood, but it is where people interact with government that the liberal link between freedom and responsibility becomes most interesting.

Liberal Democrats value the freedom that the welfare state provides: those in hardship are protected from penury. But that is not an absolute and unconditional freedom. There is no freedom to live a life of voluntary idleness paid for by others. To do so is to take the freedom the welfare state offers while ducking the obligations. So liberals also demand that people take responsibility, to do everything in their power to live independently of the state, accepting taxpayer support only for as long as they need it.

Under the previous government this social contract was stretched to breaking point. In the name of compassion, a system of means-tested entitlements was created that not only made long-term worklessness a viable option, but actively penalised those who sought to stand on their own two feet. A more infantilising, morale-sapping, disempowering system would be hard to imagine.

By decoupling freedom to receive welfare from responsibility to try and come off welfare, Labour made a serious mistake. They created an entitlement society. They removed the onus from the individual to try and be self-reliant. There was insufficient conditionality. The additional irony is that, by not requiring people to be responsible, Labour also left them less free as they ossified into a life of welfare dependency.

The debt-financed expansion of welfare that Gordon Brown oversaw at a time of economic boom created a system that bore little resemblance to the one designed by the great liberal William

Beveridge after the Second World War. Beveridge explicitly warned that 'the state, in organising security, should not stifle incentive, opportunity and responsibility'. Yet that is precisely what the system inherited by the Liberal Democrats did, and we should be proud to be reforming it.

The need for personal responsibility is at its greatest in the criminal system. After all, it is a failure to demonstrate any personal or civic responsibility that leads offenders to commit their crimes in the first place.

That is why liberals place so much emphasis not just on the use of prison as punishment, but as a place where people can be taught the importance of personal responsibility and helped to turn their lives around. That is why we have increased the amount of real work done in prisons and provided practical courses to prepare prisoners for life on the outside: literacy and numeracy classes; applied skills; and drug and alcohol therapies. And that is why we have introduced continued support for ex-offenders upon release, helping them to find a job and a suitable place to live.

Should these interventions not work – should ex-offenders fail to demonstrate the personal responsibility on which their liberty is granted and commit crime again – the sanction is clear: a return to prison.

The dilemma for liberals is what sanctions to take when people fail to take responsibility for their actions without breaking the law. People are free to smoke or drink to excess – but should they take responsibility for their subsequent ill health, and to what degree is the state responsible for treating them? People are free to spend their retirement savings as they see fit – but to what degree should the state feel obliged to help if they squander all their money?

So long as people are protected from the consequences of their actions, we risk a dangerous decoupling of rights and obligations. Such a settlement grants freedom to the individual, without any of the responsibilities that go with it. This is not a sustainable social settlement. Rather, it is a recipe for injustice and a pretext for a core

Labour assertion: that people should be denied choice because the state picks up the pieces if the choices made are bad ones.

Previous generations of liberal-minded people have down-played the responsibility of the individual in these circumstances. But people today see the freedom/responsibility equation more clearly. In Britain today there is a big appetite for helping people to help themselves; we are a decent and compassionate country. But there is little appetite for helping people who fail to help themselves; we regard this as misplaced compassion.

This is a mature understanding of liberalism: where liberty and responsibility are indivisibly linked; where people are free to make their own decisions but cannot simply walk away from the consequences.

There is also a role for a more assertive form of personal liberalism. We should not be so complacent about our freedom that we are unwilling to defend or promote it. Liberalism should not be taken for granted in Britain, nor should illiberalism be indulged, whether in Britain or internationally. There are irreducible liberal values that should be stated unequivocally.

Liberal Democrats believe in democracy. The government should derive its authority from the people and be able to be removed by the people. Liberal Democrats are vigilant about erosion of our democracy, from voter fraud to low participation rates. Most importantly, we are not willing to entertain other forms of government that do not have their legitimacy based on popular consent. So we are against autocracy and theocracy.

Liberal Democrats believe in the rule of law. Everyone is equal under the law with no favours for powerful people or special interest groups. The law is determined by parliament, elected by the people. There is no higher form of law based on military force or religious conviction.

Liberal Democrats believe in individual liberty, but that does not just include freedom from state interference. It also means people must be free from coercion based on public opinion, custom or religious preferences. So people should be free to wear traditional forms of clothing but also free not to wear traditional forms of clothing. We are against forced marriage and other forms of oppressive practice.

Liberal Democrats believe in equality between the sexes. That does not mean that every organisation must precisely employ a 50:50 ratio of men and women, but it does mean that men and women should be treated the same, without discrimination. Girls should be educated to the same standard as boys, for example. The same applies to equality for people of different ethnicities or with different sexual orientations.

Liberal Democrats believe in freedom of religious expression. We reject the punishment of apostasy. Every person should be free to decide his or her religious preferences and free to change their preferences. This freedom also extends to having no religious beliefs. People should not be discriminated against on the basis of their religious convictions or absence of them.

Liberal Democrats believe in free speech. The causing of offence is not a justification for restricting freedom of expression. We also believe in a free media. Liberal Democrats believe that progress is made through the free exchange of ideas, unsuppressed and expressed without fear.

Liberal Democrats believe in human rights. We recognise that restrictions on personal freedom are a reasonable response to an individual breaking the law, but a person who breaks the law does not forfeit all of their rights. People should be treated in a civilised manner. We reject restrictions on the human rights of people who lawfully oppose their government.

Liberal Democrats believe in civil liberties. We accept that the protection of national security is a legitimate activity for the state. That is tempered by the belief that the state is the servant of the people, not their master, and must act accordingly.

It is important that these principles are stated without ambiguity and their consistent application asserted without hesitation. They are the foundations on which our liberal civic society is built. Liberalism is a benign and generous-spirited ideology but it cannot be defenceless. If liberalism amounts to nothing more than tolerance of the intolerant, it will neither command public support nor deserve to do so.

We should be willing to assert our liberalism as the glue that holds us together as a nation, and as the example we wish to set internationally.

At a time when our growing religious and ethnic diversity prompts questions as to what it means to be British, our answer should be simple: not our flag, anthem or other symbols of nationhood. Not even our humour or our idiosyncrasies. The irreducible core of Britishness is our liberalism, and the laws and institutions that give expression to our liberal values – freedom, tolerance, equality and human rights.

And at a time when globalisation is making international law more, rather than less, important, we should be clear that although these values define us, they do not belong to us. Britain should be a beacon of light and hope for people around the world whose freedoms and rights are being abused.

Britain's liberal culture has helped to foster a remarkable climate of innovation and creativity in our country. Our values are not incidental to our national success, they are central to our future prospects. The advantages that we enjoy have not fallen on our lap – we have created them.

The industrial revolution was a product of the genius and vision of our inventors and our manufacturers. Our world-famous universities are a result of the foresight of those who valued the power of learning and ideas. Our language is the international language as a result of the spirit of adventure of travellers who explored the globe. Our political and legal systems are the result of a civic culture that demands accountability to, and a means of redress for, individual citizens.

In the fast-moving and unsentimental globalised economy, our greatest strength is our capacity for imaginative thinking. The very traits that are frowned upon in countries like China are our greatest asset.

We should cherish the cussed individualism of the British. We know our own minds and do not always like falling into line. Our children attend school not just to learn answers but also to ask questions. We should celebrate our non-conformity. It is the ability to think differently that underpins the success of everything from our military special forces to our music industry.

We should continue to question received wisdoms. Everything was new and untested once. Of course we all stand on the shoulders of our predecessors, in debt to the knowledge and experience that they accumulated, but we should reject a collectivist herd mentality: liberals are unnerved by groupthink, even when they agree with the group.

This is the mind-set of Galileo and Darwin and all the other great thinkers who questioned the settled orthodoxy of their times. And this was the mind-set that led to intellectual and philosophical advances of the Enlightenment on which modern liberal thought is founded, and on which the outcome of the ongoing battle between reason and superstition depends.

Liberalism, broadly defined, faces few out-and-out enemies here in Britain, where extremist ideologies have, mercifully, struggled to take root. The greater danger is the unreliability of its friends.

Conservatives can usually – though not always – be relied upon to side with the citizen against the state, and the individual against the collective. But they depart from liberals in the faith they place in the wisdom of our predecessors, relying on precedent, rather than reason, to guide them. Consequently, their instinct is to preserve what has gone before, not to challenge it; to resist change, not to embrace it. They are reassured, rather than discomforted, by displays of social conformity. They are relaxed about, rather than offended by, class and hierarchical structures. And the institutions they most value are those that reflect these instincts, requiring people to know their place, be cowered by convention and not to question orders.

Labour, meanwhile, are trapped by their collectivist history and purpose. The party was founded to represent a group – the workers – whose interests were to be protected by the trade unions on the shop floor and by the Labour Party in Parliament. As the size of this group has dwindled over time, so Labour has sought to represent other sections of society as well, particularly minority groups whose members' shared interests can trump their individual identities. As a consequence, Labour's ambitions to govern are dependent on their ability to nurture and maintain these group identities and to convince the groups in their collective entirety to rally behind them. Recognising that expressions of individuality (not joining your trade union) or personal ambition (buying your council house) threaten the party's power base, Labour's first instinct is to stamp them out. Collectivism runs through their veins; it is what they do.

Yet look at where Britain is globally admired. It is for our individuality and our free-thinking.

The inventor of the internet and the designer of the iPhone are British. Their creativity is transforming the world. Our industrial icons, from the Mini to the Dyson, are wonders of original thinking. The leading Formula 1 teams based in Britain draw heavily on our capacity for innovative engineering.

Our leading universities are popular with students from across the globe because they inculcate a culture of fresh ideas. Only Americans have won more Nobel prizes than Britons. Our creative industries are global leaders precisely because we are talented at being creative.

Britain can learn from other countries that are making progress. We do not do everything well. British children's core level of knowledge in maths, for example, is inferior to that of many of our competitors. Our transport infrastructure is less efficient than that in many established, as well as emerging, economies. We can do better.

But Britain's route to future success cannot be based merely on replicating the attributes of other countries. We need to address our weaknesses, but we need also to focus heavily on our core strengths, our points of competitive advantage. These strengths – our originality, subversiveness, creativity, individuality – have one big feature in common: they are the core characteristics of a liberal mind-set and a liberal society.

Britain has a remarkable evolutionary history of developing the concept of personal liberty. The general election will take place in the 800th anniversary year of Magna Carta. This should be a source of considerable national pride.

But the virtues of personal freedom should not just be understood by reference to the past. What it is to be a free person is evolving rapidly in an era of globalisation and the dramatic advance of communication technologies. This presents both threats and opportunities for free people.

In a liberal society every person should be free from an unnecessarily intrusive state. The Liberal Democrats have been the strongest and most consistent advocates of civil liberties in British politics.

The Labour government proposed a series of draconian measures in the name of collective security. These included extending to ninety days the period over which a suspect could be detained before being charged with an offence, as well as the introduction of identity cards. The attitude towards these measures illustrates neatly the difference between Labour's authoritarian instincts and the liberal alternative.

The Liberal Democrats regarded ninety days' detention as grossly excessive. There clearly needs to be a period during which a suspect can be detained and questioned. But the suspect has not been found guilty, or even charged with anything, and should not be treated as if he or she were guilty. It is a hallmark of the most oppressive states when people are locked up for an extended period without any proof that an offence has been committed.

The Liberal Democrats also opposed identity cards. There were practical and financial considerations but our opposition was based on principle. The balance between the individual and the state would have been subtly but substantially altered. Liberal Democrats believe the state serves the people, not the other way round. An individual should not have to justify him or herself to the state when there is no evidence of wrong-doing. It should be possible for a person to walk down the street without being stopped and detained if not in possession of the correct documentation.

The Liberal Democrats have also had to remain vigilant against Conservative authoritarianism. The Conservative Party is an uneasy coalition of libertarians and authoritarians, with the latter normally in the ascendency. In this parliament, the Liberal Democrats have prevented a major extension of the power of the state to monitor and collect data on the private communications of individuals. We believe that it is wrong for every person to live under a cloud of permanent suspicion, not knowing the degree to which the state is intruding into the most personal aspects of their life.

The growth in technology still makes it increasingly easy for the state and for private businesses to monitor our private lives. Mobile phone and internet browser records, satellite imagery, CCTV and loyalty cards all paint a picture of our interests, movements and activities.

While there is a role for the properly authorised and targeted use of surveillance to catch serious criminals and terrorists, we cannot allow the promise of enhanced security to justify an untrammelled role for the state. And while businesses can legitimately use data to improve their efficiency and customer service, it is reasonable to have safeguards to protect against the abuse of information.

Liberals have an instinctive unease about the degree to which technology is curtailing individual freedom. Authoritarians do not.

Those who cherish the freedom of the individual – and believe we cannot defend our liberty by forfeiting our liberties – have a natural ally in the Liberal Democrats.

It would, however, be a great mistake to see the internet and other forms of information and communication technology only as a threat to personal freedom. They are also an exciting and liberating new force.

They provide remarkable new opportunities for human interaction. Where once people could interact only with others in their village, today they can interact with all of humanity. Companies that started by trading in a literal marketplace now trade in a global marketplace. The scope for enhanced knowledge, understanding and prosperity is enormous.

The opportunity for free people to hold the powerful to account, including their own government, is also far greater. In Britain the volume of government information online, from hospital performance indicators to council tax charges, has the potential to transform the role of the citizen from passive bystander to empowered consumer. That in turn has the potential to drive up standards as service providers become more accountable and services more responsive and personalised. The nature of the relationship between the governed and the governing is evolving. The citizen has never been better equipped.

Authoritarian countries are fearful of these changes. They are right to be. In the short term, they can seek to clamp down even harder, blocking websites, monitoring communications, banning broadcasts, but they will struggle to hold back the tide forever. The democratic power of the internet can only be resisted for so long.

Even in liberal democracies, governments and wider society are having to adjust quickly to the new era of instantaneous, global communications, and some of the policy responses have been slow-footed. But this is an exciting new process that is in its relative infancy. With this debate the direction of travel is clear. The opportunities for extending personal freedom are opening up; what it is to be a free person is expanding. That is exhilarating for liberals. It is also fundamental to the freedom, security and prosperity of the British people.

The politicians in the other parties are more wary. Their reference points are the politics of social class and the nation state. The former is irrelevant to this debate and the latter is only of tangential relevance. How globalisation, powered by technological advance, can extend prosperity, democracy and freedom is a fundamentally liberal discussion.

Giving the other parties responsibility for this transformational agenda in 2015 is like giving a mechanic a manual written in an unfamiliar foreign language. He may look willing, have a go at getting your vehicle on the road, and will almost certainly take your money, but the drive towards greater personal freedom and the protection of individual liberty is best undertaken by the party that designed the car.

The only party that truly understands the liberal age and the opportunities it presents for a liberal country, is the Liberal Democrats. The clue is in the name.

Chapter 3

Opportunity

The purpose of liberalism is to promote freedom and, by extension, opportunity.

There is straightforward freedom from oppression, intrusion and interference. This could be called 'Freedom from...', and it concerns the ability of free people to live their lives as they see fit.

But liberalism also recognises that, for most people, there are significant constraints on their freedom unless barriers to their progress are lowered or removed. This could be called 'Freedom to...' and it revolves around the notion of capability. It suggests that the role of the state is to empower people so that they can achieve everything they are capable of achieving.

It was this realisation that true liberty involves positive, as well as negative, freedoms that motivated previous generations of liberals to champion great social changes. A person who is illiterate or innumerate is not truly free. That person may be protected from the arbitrary power of a malign state or other organisation, but his or her life remains limited, the potential unrealised.

Victorian reformers responded to this need for an active liberalism by providing educational opportunities for children from poor backgrounds. All people, regardless of circumstances, would have the opportunity at the start of their life to explore their talents and achieve their ambitions. It was an exhilarating era of social reform.

In 2015 the Liberal Democrat goal is to dismantle the barriers that still stand between too many of our citizens and the jobs they could do, the money they could earn, the lives they could lead.

The starting point for achieving this goal must be education. It is the key that unlocks the door to opportunity. It is the surest route to a more socially mobile and meritocratic society.

Britain's education system does not provide opportunity for all – far from it. Only a minority of our young people acquire the knowledge and skills of which they are capable. As a result, we are, as a nation, moving at half-power, and are rapidly being overtaken by our competitors. The PISA global rankings show the United Kingdom ranked twenty-sixth for maths, twenty-third for reading and twenty-first for science. Singapore, Hong Kong, South Korea and Japan scored in the top ten in all three categories.

When the big issue of our time is globalisation and the rise of Asia, this represents a huge competitive disadvantage. Britain cannot succeed in an intensely competitive global economy without maximising the ability of every person. This is a whole team effort – we need everyone to contribute.

Yet in 2013 the Organisation for Economic Co-operation and Development (OECD) revealed that England is the only country in the developed world in which numeracy and literacy standards among 16- to 24-year-olds were no better than among 55- to 65-year-olds. So in two generations we have stood still. Every other developed country has progressed. This is a sobering fact.

Even more shockingly, the performance of children from poor backgrounds is much worse still. Forty-one per cent of all children failed to achieve five GCSE A*–C grades including English and maths in 2013; for children poor enough to qualify for free school meals this figure was 62 per cent – almost two thirds of this cohort fell short of what should be seen as the bare minimum level of attainment.

The need to raise overall education standards has motivated

the Liberal Democrats in government to undertake a series of far-reaching reforms.

Teachers have been given more freedom and schools more autonomy as the number of academy schools has proliferated and as new 'free schools', founded by parents, teachers, community groups and others, have been established. This has extended parental choice and increased competition, which in turn has spurred innovation and driven up standards. Uniformity and stasis have been replaced by diversity and dynamism; examples of what can be done, even in the most deprived communities, have seen expectations rise and aspirations soar.

Reflecting the priority that Liberal Democrats attach to education, the schools budget has been protected in a period when other budgets have necessarily had to be reduced. To do otherwise would have saved a little in the short term, but would have been costly for Britain in the long run. Of all the investments a government can make, the effective education of young people is by far the most important.

The system by which schools are held accountable for their performance has also been overhauled. Under the Labour government, a school was deemed to be failing if fewer than 30 per cent of its pupils achieved five GCSEs at C grade or better. This encouraged schools to focus their efforts on those children on the C/D grade borderline, to teach them the subjects that were easiest to pass, to narrow the curriculum to just the subjects that 'counted', and then to teach those subjects 'to the test'. Pupils were given just enough knowledge to pass an exam, but not enough to acquire or demonstrate a deeper understanding of the subject.

Today, all of these defects have been addressed. The performance of a secondary school is judged on the progress the pupils make relative to their results aged eleven, with the progress made by every pupil counting equally. To reflect the importance of the core skills of literacy and numeracy – the foundation upon which all other academic study stands – double weight is given to English and maths results in the calculations. To prevent schools from entering pupils for those exams that are deemed easiest to pass, pupils are now assessed by how well they perform over eight subjects, rather than five, and there is a requirement that three of these subjects (in addition to English and maths) be strictly academic ones (the sciences, humanities and modern languages). Furthermore, to ensure that qualifications truly reflect the understanding that a pupil has of their subject matter, module-based coursework has, where appropriate, been replaced by exams, while the exams have been made less predictable and harder to 'game'.

All pupils will benefit from these reforms, but the biggest winners will be the young people not near the C/D grade borderline, who were previously of only marginal importance to head teachers and teachers, whose first priority, not unreasonably, was to avoid the sack that could result if government targets were not met.

Perhaps most important of all, however, has been the extra attention devoted to addressing the under-achievement of children from low-income households. The Liberal Democrat 'pupil premium' has targeted extra funding at children eligible for free school meals. The intention has been to help schools provide disadvantaged children with the extra support they need to succeed. In keeping with our liberal instincts, head teachers have been given discretion to spend this money as they see fit. The schools have freedom to exercise professional judgement; the government holds them to account for their results. Encouragingly, those results are now beginning to move in the right direction. Average attainment is going up overall, but those pupils in receipt of the 'pupil premium' are seeing their results rise the fastest. The link between poverty and educational failure is, at long last, beginning to weaken.

It is easier for children to keep up than to catch up, which is why the first years of a child's life are so crucial to their future prospects. So that is why the 'pupil premium' is weighted towards primary schools (where it is worth £1,300 per child, compared to £900 in secondary schools). It is also why the Liberal Democrats have made fifteen hours of high quality pre-school education available to all three- and four-year-olds and the poorest 40 per cent of two-year-olds. And it is why we have introduced an 'early-years pupil premium' that channels more resources towards pre-school children from low-income families. And it is why, on top of all this, the Liberal Democrats are, from this autumn, providing every five-, six- and seven-year-old with a free nutritious lunch – trials of which showed significant benefits for all pupils' attainment, particularly the poorest.

While we have made a good start, we are still in the early stages of the journey that is required if we are to liberate the potential of every young person and ensure that Britain is able to compete in the global economy.

So we will continue to raise the bar on school standards. We will continue to support our highest-achieving schools, while acting swiftly and decisively to address failure. And we will go on doing so until every school is rated good or outstanding, and England's education system is once again at the top of the world league tables.

And as we continue to raise our expectations of our schools, so we will also increase the support we give them. In the next parliament, we will expand the protection afforded to the schools budget so that it also covers pre-school and sixth form. And we will continue to provide more than £2.5 billion every year specifically to provide additional support to the poorest pupils, so that they can reap the benefits that their more affluent peers often receive at home – one-to-one tuition, out-of-hours instruction, extra-curricular activities and horizon-expanding visits. At every step of every child's journey to adulthood, we will do whatever it takes to help each of them fulfil their potential.

A controversial decision in this parliament was to increase the student tuition fees that Labour introduced. No mainstream party is proposing to abolish student fees, so the task in 2015 is to continue to ensure that higher education is available to all and that British universities provide excellent levels of teaching.

It is encouraging for liberals that the number of people from poorer backgrounds going to university has continued to rise – with numbers of students from low-income families now at record levels. This has not happened by accident, but as a direct result of the progressive student funding system we have introduced, which, for many, has actually reduced the cost of going to university even as fees have gone up. Indeed, no graduate is now required to repay their student loan until they are earning over £21,000 (up from £15,000 under Labour). That so many young people recognise the benefit of going to university is testament to the value that they attach to learning and to the importance employers continue to attach to degree-level qualifications.

Britain has some of the best universities in the world. They are a great national asset and a powerful stimulator of social mobility. They now have a sustainable and secure funding model which does not leave them competing with all the other demands for public spending that can seem more important, more urgent, or both. The funding system should also make students more discerning about the quality and quantity of the teaching that they receive, which in turn should make universities more responsive to student demands. This is a positive development: more empowered individuals, with higher expectations, better able to shape their university experience.

This is the Liberal Democrat record: better early-years provision; more money for schools; choice for parents; more autonomy for heads; more freedom for teachers; more help for children from disadvantaged backgrounds; more rigorous exams; a more sophisticated accountability system; and greater access to our world-class universities.

Clearing the deficit is the unavoidable task. But continuing to build an education system that can unlock the potential of all our young people is the most important task – and a central feature of the Liberal Democrat offer for 2015.

The welfare state is widely valued as a safety net for people who need support. It is a basic hallmark of a decent society that vulnerable people are spared the prospect of destitution.

The task in 2015, however, is to continue to re-shape the welfare state so that it not only provides security, but also expands the life chances of its recipients. The annual cost of the welfare state is £120 billion (excluding pensions); the goal is to make sure that this enormous sum of money works to create opportunity for all.

That is not to disregard the safety-net aspect of the welfare state; when somebody falls it is important to catch them – after all, any of us can, at any moment, become disabled, fall ill, or be made redundant. But we should not be content just to catch people who have fallen; we should aspire to help them back onto their feet.

The Labour model of welfare failed. Even when the economy was growing strongly a decade ago, welfare bills continued to rise inexorably. The disconcerting notion of a welfare under-class – barely a concept in Britain in previous generations – established itself in the '80s and took root under Labour.

Conservative economic changes in the '80s led to high levels of unemployment for people previously occupied in manual jobs. The modernisation of the economy – necessary and inevitable – left large numbers of people unnecessarily behind. Some found new jobs, but many others were made to feel redundant, not just from paid employment but also from the needs of the country. They became the long-term unemployed – a welfare class rather than a working class.

This was a grim inheritance for Labour, but their approach came to compound, rather than rectify, the problems of the people they purported to serve. The long-term unemployed, and increasing numbers of never-employed, were parked on welfare: out-of-sight and out-of-mind. To keep the unemployment figures down, huge numbers of people were put on sickness and disability benefits, signed off and effectively abandoned. They often lived separate lives from the working population, in different communities and with different ambitions.

Labour focused their attention, and huge amounts of government money, on the symptoms of the problem, not the fundamental causes. Those deep causes of this terrible human malaise – lack of skills and opportunities – were neglected in favour of trying to shift hundreds of thousands of people out of a theoretical definition of poverty while leaving their lives essentially untouched. Statistically, the problem was diminished; in reality, their lives continued largely unchanged.

The Labour assumption was that poverty could be solved by giving more welfare money to poor people. No reasonable person would claim that poverty has nothing to do with money, and a small increase in benefit levels does ease the squeeze on family budgets a little, but what it does not do is fundamentally alter someone's current predicament or future prospects. An extra £10 may put a little more food on the table, but it does not improve a person's skill levels or job prospects. All too often, the welfare system encouraged dependency and penalised self-help.

This is the problem with the top-down, clunking, uniform view that Labour has of society. If poverty is defined as being below 60 per cent of median earnings, then for large numbers of people at 55–60 per cent of median earnings poverty can be 'solved' by giving them enough money to push them just over the line. Indeed, it can even be 'solved' if median earnings fall, as has happened in the recent recession, pushing the poverty line down. In this 'through the looking glass' world, a person's income and circumstances can remain unaltered, yet they cease to be classified

as poor because those above them on the income scale have seen
their earnings fall.

Labour are understandably indignant that the more cynical Conservatives disregard the plight of the poorest people, believing them
to be irredeemably committed to voting Labour or unlikely to vote
at all. But Labour's failing is to see people always in categories, ripe
for mass statistical manipulation, rather than as individuals with
unique needs and ambitions.

So this was the Liberal Democrat inheritance in 2010. People living
in households where nobody had ever worked, the idea of working
totally alien to them. People with no incentive to be self-reliant,
their ambition snuffed out, their self-esteem drained away. Millions
of people caught in a web of means-testing, made worse-off if they
took a job or worked additional hours, rewarded if they organised
their circumstances in such a way as to maximise their entitlement.

That is why the Liberal Democrats have sought to rebalance the
government's poverty strategy to focus on education and employment – the best way of breaking the cycle that sees poor children
grow up to be poor adults. It is why, to inform a more intelligent
policy response, we will add two new measures of poverty to the
existing one based on 60 per cent of median income. One will focus
on life chances, defined by educational attainment; the other on
entrenched poverty – those who are at greatest risk, due to unemployment or other factors, not just of being poor, but of remaining
poor long term.

And it is why we have reformed the welfare system to ensure that
work always pays, providing additional support for, and making
additional demands of, every unemployed person who is capable
of work. And it is working. With the exception of housing benefit,
which continues to rise in-line with rents, spending on all the major
working-age benefits is on a downwards trajectory, with job-seekers,
single parents and recipients of incapacity benefit all moving into
the labour market. We have been compassionate enough to give

people adequate benefits and compassionate enough not to leave them on benefits when that is not necessary or desirable.

Welfare reform cannot succeed in the longer term if the economy is not growing, which is why our determination to stick to the government's economic plan, even as our opponents were urging us to abandon it, has been the single biggest anti-poverty measure we have implemented. Two million private sector jobs have been created. That is two million people getting paid; two million people with the sense of self-worth that comes from self-reliance; two million people who are now less dependent or no longer dependent on the state.

The challenge now is to continue this progress. The Liberal Democrats will always ensure the welfare state provides a real bulwark against penury, but we will not measure our success or seek to demonstrate our moral virtue by the cost and apparent generosity of the system. An enlightened and compassionate society is not one that creates dependency, but one that frees people from it.

And not all the costs of welfare are negative: some public spending encourages and incentivises work. The provision of childcare, for example, enables people, particularly women, to return to employment.

That is why we have expanded the number of free hours of childcare available to pre-school children and why we have introduced a £2,000-a-year 'tax-free childcare scheme' to help working families with costs. This is on top of the childcare support already provided through the tax credit system.

It is also why we have introduced a system of shared parental leave so that parents have more flexibility to decide how, together, they will balance the demands of raising a child with their ambitions to work and maintain a reasonable household income. This change will have a big and lasting cultural impact, allowing fathers to spend more time with their babies, while significantly increasing opportunities for women in the workplace.

Most importantly, opportunity for people in Britain depends on our country being globally competitive. The biggest factor is a successful economy. Expanding businesses have bigger budgets to hire, train and develop staff. They have more money to spend on new technology, research and development, driving up productivity.

And, again, the government can make a positive contribution. Government support for science has been protected even during a period of austerity in recognition of the importance of innovation to our future national productivity. Extra effort has been devoted to assisting businesses keen to export to the fast-expanding markets. Improved infrastructure is helping to underpin economic success. A more international, prosperous and ambitious Britain will create new opportunities.

For those of retirement age, opportunity takes different forms. Many people are choosing to continue in work, often by preference rather than due to financial necessity. Some enjoy staying in work part-time – keeping active, making a contribution, enjoying the company of colleagues, bringing in helpful extra income.

The Liberal Democrats have been at the forefront of this process of encouraging flexible retirement. It is a great liberal freedom to be able to determine the scope and duration of your own working life. A million people in Britain over the age of sixty-five are economically active today, an increase of almost 50 per cent in just five years. The idea of people being too old to work, in an age of dramatically increased life expectancy, already feels anachronistic.

For those who have finished work, active retirement can bring great pleasure and personal satisfaction. It is an opportunity for personal development, trying new activities, contributing to the community and travelling to new places. The recently retired form the backbone of voluntary Britain. When a retired person visits a school to read with a disadvantaged child the lives of both participants are enriched.

Enjoying the opportunities of retirement is helped by having a reasonable income. Liberal Democrats have been at the forefront of encouraging saving for retirement, simplifying financial products to make them more consumer-friendly and reduce the scope for customer exploitation. We have introduced a default assumption into pension savings schemes which leaves employees free to choose not to save but results in more people making provision for their retirement. And we have introduced the state pension 'triple-lock' to ensure that the relative living standards of those who are already retired and depend on the state pension do not fall behind those of the working population.

As Liberal Democrats, we welcome all these trends across different sections of society. We want to challenge the idea that a person can be a parent or a worker, but cannot be both. We want to challenge the idea that, on a given calendar date, working life must end and retirement begins. We want to challenge the idea that people with disabilities cannot work and make a contribution. And we want to challenge the idea that children from poor families cannot end up at the very best universities, that it is impossible to break the link between material deprivation and educational failure.

This is the optimistic, dynamic, opportunity society that the Liberal Democrats believe in.

The problem with having a commitment to opportunity for all is that it risks sounding like a promise of motherhood and apple pie. After all, no political party claims to be *against* opportunity for all, no politician argues that people should be *prevented* from reaching their full potential.

Despite this, I believe that extending opportunity is a distinctly liberal mission which, if delivered, would shatter the established social order, the maintenance of which suits both the other parties.

Labour feels uncomfortable about policies that, by helping people climb the ladder of opportunity, risk turning solid 'Labour people' into aspirational middle-class voters who might vote for another party. That is why Labour has never fully reconciled itself to 'free schools' and academies, or the 'right to buy' policy for council house tenants, or the idea of a share-owning democracy, or radical welfare reform. Labour is an explicitly class-based party, established by the trade unions to represent the interests of the working class in parliament. The smaller the working class becomes, the greater the anxiety in the Labour Party about the future of the Labour Party.

For Labour opportunity is not for all – there is always a zero-sum calculation. The party is most comfortable with battles where one side of society wins and the other side loses. In economic debates Labour is more interested in gaining a bigger share of the cake for their voters than increasing the size of the cake for all voters. Indeed, they usually give the impression that they could live with a smaller cake so long as they increase their share.

Labour's collectivism also makes them suspicious of the idea of personal advancement. They are the party of uniformity: where Liberal Democrats seek equality of opportunity, Labour aim for equality of outcome. Labour's notion of equality makes them antipathetic to every person having the chance to maximise his or her potential; personal growth is resented when it threatens to exceed the prescribed norm. It is such a stunting and depressing ideology, so out-of-tune with human nature, that the only times Labour have won a general election in the last forty years, under Tony Blair, they succeeded only by downplaying it.

Meanwhile, the Conservatives are prepared to follow the logic of their rhetorical commitment to opportunity only to the point at which it starts to threaten their own supporter base. Their willingness to tackle disadvantage is conditional on not questioning the inherited privilege and patronage that can stand as a barrier to progress. So, at the last election, while the Liberal Democrat priority was income tax cuts for people on normal incomes, the Conservatives preferred inheritance tax cuts which would have benefitted richer households. The Conservatives are not against the idea of people climbing the ladder, but their real priority, it often seems, is to stop those at the top from slipping down it.

Most Conservatives are motivated to protect the status quo from the threat posed by opportunity being extended to everyone. The party is, by instinct, the upholder of the established social order. This tendency runs deep in their collective mind-set. Even when there is some modest social churn there remains a subtle hierarchy in the minds of Conservatives, a delineation between the 'old money' establishment and the 'new money' *arrivistes*, with their unrefined and gauche pretensions.

Conservatives, as the name makes clear, are in the preservation business. The party is instinctively resistant to change. It finds greatest comfort in the past. That is why Conservatives most value the institutions that evoke a dated Britishness – they offer reassuring familiarity.

It is hard to reconcile the notion of opportunity for all with these Conservative traits. Everyone being able to achieve their full potential requires a fluid, dynamic society, not a stiff, settled social order. It means the most talented and industrious people need to be able to rise without impediment. It also means that the relatively untalented or idle should not retain the highest positions of authority based on their family heritage.

Class-based politics suits Labour and the Conservatives. It creates the safe seats for their politicians: Wigan for Labour, Tunbridge Wells for the Conservatives. It divides the country: north and south; urban and rural; rich and poor.

There are politicians in both parties who recognise the sterility of class-based politics and its growing irrelevance to modern Britain. They provide fertile ground for constructive, non-tribal collaboration with the Liberal Democrats. But they remain outnumbered and culturally ostracised in parties that would happily return to the class-based politics that resonated in Britain fifty years ago. That is why the concept of opportunity for all is distinctive to the Liberal Democrats. We are not a party defined by an allegiance to one social class and opposition to another. It does not matter to us where a person went to school, what accent they speak with, their ethnicity, or any other categorisation. What matters are their innate talents and abilities, not their membership of a client group.

That is why, when liberals talk about opportunity for all, we actually mean it. For that is what liberalism is: the freedom to be who you are; the opportunity to be who you could be.

Chapter 4

Decentralisation

The goal for liberals is to transfer power from remote institutions to individuals and communities. We do not believe in 'Big Government'; we believe in 'Big People'.

The relationship between the governed and the governing is changing. The way that democracy has worked in the past will not work in the future. We are living in the liberal age. So much has already changed, from social attitudes to the shape of the workplace. It is inconceivable that the liberal tide will not reach our institutions of Parliament and government.

Liberalism is the belief in freedom – confident, emancipated citizens, not cowering masses. So Liberal Democrats have always been at the forefront of constitutional innovation. The relationship between the state and the individual goes to the heart of our ideology. For the other parties, decisions about the structures of politics are marginal. For Liberal Democrats this subject is fundamental; it is about who holds power.

It would be a mistake to believe that we in Britain have reached the evolutionary end point of politics, yet that is a widely held delusion. We have gone through the stages of development, extending the electoral franchise to larger numbers of people. We have the 'Mother of Parliaments' and a mature collective understanding of the civic underpinning of democracy. We have become accustomed to the rituals of our system: voting on a Thursday; late-night election declarations; Cabinet appointees shuffling in and out of Downing Street; Prime Minister's Questions. The unchanging character of our political system is, we tell ourselves, evidence of its enduring strength.

Yet the world beyond Westminster is changing, even if the established approach to government and politics is not. At the 1951 general election, Labour and the Conservatives, between them, got 97 per cent of the vote. At that time, our politics was an accurate reflection of our society: two monolithic class-based blocks. Since then society has evolved dramatically. It is more fluid, more dynamic and less deferential and, as people's political views have become more complex and their allegiances less predictable, so the vote for the two old class-based parties has tumbled.

When I was first elected in 2005 the combined Labour–Conservative vote fell below 70 per cent for the first time since the war. When I was re-elected in 2010 it fell to a new record low of 65 per cent. Even with an electoral system designed to corral the voters into two camps, over a third of those voting decided to reject the established bi-polar order. In the 2014 European Parliament elections, albeit under a different voting system, the Labour–Conservative joint vote was 49 per cent.

Society is losing interest in politics-as-usual. Election turnouts are often dismal. Political party membership has collapsed. Political donors are frequently stigmatised rather than admired for their generous civic dispensation. Politicians are widely mistrusted. Indeed, somewhat perversely, the public typically hold officials whom they have not chosen in higher esteem than the politicians whom they have chosen.

This process seems likely to accelerate. It is not just a storm that politicians can hope to weather. Some anger towards politicians may dissipate as economic circumstances improve, but indifference and apathy are likely to endure. At a time when people have never been so empowered or presented with so much choice, in almost all aspects of their lives, voters are unsurprisingly turned off by the stifling narrowness of class-based identity politics.

As a democrat, I think the crisis of faith in politics is deeply concerning. But these changing attitudes should not be seen as being unambiguously problematic. The old order – patronising, arrogant, aloof and sectional – has run out of road. There is little point lamenting its demise. Whether it is good or bad is, to a large extent, irrelevant – it is happening. The task is to find the right response.

There is no single change that will restore faith in politics. We can be certain that empty gimmicks aimed at tapping into the latest zeitgeist will fail. The success of politics in the liberal age requires politicians who genuinely understand the nature of changing public attitudes. We need a new politics which goes with the grain of our new society and which recasts the relationship between the governed and the governing. The Liberal Democrat instinct for empowering the individual has never been more relevant.

The essential precondition for reinventing our politics is to understand that the process is necessary. Most people would be anxious to discover that the core assumptions on which they built their lives and careers no longer held true – and the same is true for most politicians. When such a conclusion can no longer be denied, the temptation is to search for superficial responses which give the impression of change while actually preserving the status quo. That will be the approach of many politicians in 2015.

This temptation will be strongest for those politicians who have most to lose from change. Labour and the Conservatives believe they have a right to govern alone. They have clung to this view even as they have each seen their support ebb away to around a third of those who bother to vote. Understandably, they hark after the certainties of the old class-based order where the two parties took it in turn to govern.

Although there is no silver bullet that will address our political malaise, a useful place to start is by looking at the electoral system which sustains our increasingly dated two-party political infrastructure.

There is no perfect electoral system. One benefit of the existing system is the link between the individual MP and his or her constituency. It personalises what can otherwise be an impersonal relationship between the individual and the state, and it improves accountability. Nearly every other electoral system, to varying degrees, would diminish this link.

So it is more helpful to reflect on what an election – and an electoral system – is designed to achieve. British general elections allow people to choose both a government (indirectly) and their own Member of Parliament (directly). Supporters of the status quo – including both Labour and the Conservatives – argue that the existing system provides strong one-party government. The problem with their argument is two-fold. One: it is no longer true. Two: the appetite for one party to provide its version of strong government has waned.

What we are saddled with, as a result, is an electoral system which horribly disfigures the will of the electorate. In an era of greater consumer choice it is an anachronism. The votes of significant sections of the population – UKIP supporters, for example – are effectively disregarded. The business-as-usual politicians assume that just because those views are not represented in the House of Commons they do not exist. But they do, and those who hold them rightly resent being ignored. What is more, the system requires even the two old class-based parties to mask their own internal divisions in order to hold their own uneasy coalitions together. Tony Blair shares almost no beliefs with members of the Labour left while many politicians on the Conservative right have more in common with UKIP than they do with their own leader.

To carry on as if the existing arrangement accurately reflects popular opinion is to treat the electorate with contempt.

When the referendum on the Alternative Vote was lost in 2011, most commentators assumed the decades-long campaign for electoral reform, led by the Liberal Democrats, had reached its natural end. Since then, however, three-party politics has, with the rise of UKIP, turned into four-party politics, yet we are about to hold another election under a system designed for the old two-party system. In all likelihood, millions of new voters are about to experience the political alienation that disenfranchisement breeds and which Liberal Democrat voters know only too well. In a proportional system, UKIP would receive between thirty and sixty-five seats if it were to receive between 5 and 10 per cent of the vote. Under first-past-the-post, it is possible that the party will win no seats at all.

In retrospect, supporters of electoral reform may come to regard the rejection of the Alternative Vote as being the right verdict, albeit arrived at for the wrong reasons. The Alternative Vote is a modification of the status quo, not an acceptance that the status quo is no longer adequate. It is a sticking plaster and it would not have held for long.

So the Liberal Democrat campaign for genuine electoral reform will continue. Not, as our opponents have long claimed, out of self-interest, but on behalf of the third of voters who regularly vote for a party other than Labour or the Conservatives and who find their votes disregarded and their views ignored. And, even more importantly, in a liberal age characterised by individual empowerment and choice, the limiting and miserably disempowering system we still have is no longer in tune with our requirements. It should not be that controversial to believe that the way people vote should be reflected in the outcome. Proportional representation is not itself sufficient to bring about the new politics, but it is necessary.

It will also be necessary to completely overhaul the House of Lords. It is extraordinary that, of the three largest parties, only the Liberal Democrats unambiguously hold this position.

The composition of the House of Lords is indefensible. It contains politicians who have tried repeatedly to get elected to Parliament and failed alongside politicians who were specifically ejected by the electorate from the House of Commons and put straight into the House of Lords instead. It contains major party donors who have effectively bought a seat in our national legislature. It draws on the retired civil service and quangocratic elite who have presumed throughout their working lives to make decisions that affect people without troubling themselves to seek any consent from those same people. And it has some hereditary members whose membership is dependent on the status of their father. That this last criterion is increasingly used by Labour to select their general election candidates does not make it any more acceptable for the House of Lords.

The House of Lords is another walking advertisement for the contempt with which the political elite hold the general public. I do not doubt that many of its members are possessed by a spirit of public service. That is a good reason for them to volunteer to do charitable work. It is not a good reason for them to decide the laws of the country that the rest of us have to obey.

It matters less precisely what form a replacement for the House of Lords takes than that it is replaced. During this parliament Labour and Conservative MPs blocked a Liberal Democrat proposal to substantially reform the House of Lords. Even that proposal contained compromises to placate those who see nothing wrong with maintaining the status quo. Perhaps the reformers who want to reconnect politics to the changing mood of the people will benefit from painting in more vivid primary colours.

Another exemplar of out-of-touch, disconnected politics is the European Union. It is perfectly possible to believe in the benefits of cooperation with other countries in Europe and still despair at the anti-democratic culture of the EU.

The institutions of the EU are designed to ensure that the journey towards 'ever closer union' is not derailed by popular opposition. So the president of the EU Commission and the president of the EU Council have no genuine democratic mandate. They are removed and detached from the people of Europe. When the population of any given European country vote in a referendum against further institutional integration they are ignored and expected to try again until they vote the other way.

Even the European Parliament, which is directly elected, lacks legitimacy. That is because there is no genuine pan-European polity. The different national parties in the socialist group have differing standpoints; the same applies to the Christian Democrat and Liberal groupings. Even UKIP represents a different strand of nationalism from the other nationalist parties. The result is a body that has the trappings of a parliament – debates and votes – but without the umbilical link to the populace that makes a genuine parliament a forum for the expression of the public will.

The widespread alienation of the British people from the EU project is a serious blight on our democracy. The gulf between the governed and the governing is enormous. That plenty of leading lights in the EU regard this as a virtue rather than a critical weakness only under lines the extent of the problem.

In 2015 the Liberal Democrats stand for Britain's continued membership of the EU but with a commitment to substantial reform. It cannot be right for democrats to suspend their critical faculties when it comes to the functioning of the EU. The winds of change are blowing through every institution – they should certainly pass through Brussels.

Most people regard a referendum on Britain's membership as inevitable, even if the precise timing is a matter for debate. That is unsurprising given how much the EU has changed as an institution since the British people voted to join the common market forty years ago. As with the wider crisis of public confidence in politics, ignoring this issue will not make it disappear.

When institutional changes next require Britain to take stock of our relationship with the EU, the Liberal Democrats will hold an In/Out referendum.

Extending freedom also requires power to be put closer to the people.

Britain is too centralised. The government in London is too controlling. The result is that people feel detached from the decisions that shape their lives.

Central government has obvious functions that cannot be delegated – macro-economic policy, foreign policy, defence and national security chief among them.

But Whitehall has extended itself way beyond these core functions. Central government refuses to allow elected councillors to set the council tax beyond narrowly confined national criteria. It even – absurdly – seeks to impose a uniform approach to the frequency of local bin collections.

The government has also eased some restrictions on local councils, but the centralising instinct continues to be exhibited by both Conservative and Labour politicians. Conservatives yearn to emasculate Labour-controlled councils, while their suspicion of the culture within the public services can lead them to be highly directive in areas like education. Labour, meanwhile, make a virtue of standardisation. When leading Labour politicians rail against a 'postcode lottery' what they are complaining about is local people having the freedom to be creative, think innovatively or seek to raise their performance. The idea that local communities might wish to set local priorities to meet local needs and wishes remains an alien concept to them. In the minds of Labour, uniform mediocrity always trumps uneven excellence.

Liberalism has a different emphasis. Liberal Democrats are driven less by what we can do for people and more by what we can help people do for themselves. We are not seeking to control every outcome. We do not assume that what works best for one part of the country must always work best for every part of the country. Liberal Democrats recognise that imposing uniformity crushes creativity. We have an instinctive belief in the value of diversity. We do not believe that to be different is to be wrong.

This makes the Liberal Democrats ideally equipped to understand how the distribution of power within the United Kingdom can best be aligned to the changing nature of the relationship between the governed and the governing.

There needs to be a renaissance in our non-Whitehall levels of government. There has already been extensive, though asymmetric, devolution to Scotland, Wales and Northern Ireland. 'Devo-Max' will take this process further in Scotland. And there has been some decentralisation within England too, but with the delegation of financial and other decision-making powers must now come a shift in culture. The big cities, which did so much to drive the progress of the Victorian age, should not view themselves as administrators of central government programmes and welfare entitlements, but as drivers of local economic growth. Their politicians should be judged by whether they succeeded in making their city more prosperous and attractive, not on whether they extracted more largess from London.

Local councils should be fulcrums for new ideas. They should be pioneers. They should draw on the talents of a wide range of interested people. This will not be achievable without reform to local government. As well as being less cowered by national government and having greater freedom, the system for electing councillors needs to change to reflect the diversity of potential contributions within any given community.

It is not a coincidence that many weaker councils are one-party fiefdoms. Competition improves performance; lack of accountability breeds complacency. When a council has every single councillor elected from the same party, on a low turnout, despite significant support for other political opinions, it is hardly surprising when the performance of the council is uninspiring.

So the Liberal Democrats propose a proportional voting system for councils too. That will disadvantage the Liberal Democrats in some areas, but there are wider considerations than party-political advantage. A plurality of opinions is healthy. Even the most decisive political leaders benefit from having their ideas tested and improved by others who are not wholly like-minded.

In addition to being able to see a correlation between their interests and the ability of the council to make meaningful decisions that reflect those interests, the voters need to see a correlation between their participation and the outcome. This is an easily achievable reform and it is essential. That only the Liberal Democrats of the three largest parties take this view shows how difficult it will be to prise open the old political vested interests and allow instead the public a greater stake in the decision-making process.

The changes I have described so far are to existing institutions. They are radical and would have a dramatic impact. They would constitute the biggest shift in power from the governing to the governed in living memory. It is a distinctive and important Liberal Democrat policy platform in 2015. But they are, nevertheless, changes to the existing order.

What politicians will also have to show a willingness to consider is additional and more fundamental change. People are becoming more discerning and promiscuous political customers. Fewer voters have an unshakeable attachment to a single political party. Even in the past twenty years this has changed significantly. It used to be common for people to feel a sense of obligation to vote for the party supported by their parents and grandparents. Political allegiances possessed almost a sense of hereditary identity. That is rarer now.

At present all the legitimacy of the national government rests on the votes cast every five years in constituency-wide elections. In 2015 most MPs will not receive the majority of votes in their constituency. The largest party in the House of Commons will receive nothing like the majority of votes cast nationally (it may not even receive the most votes). Then the political bandwagon rolls on for five more years without formal reference to the public. It feels harder to sustain.

I do not think that any political party has the absolute solution to this democratic legitimacy deficit. Maybe there is no absolute solution. Different political ideas are floating around. The right to recall errant MPs has a symbolic virtue but its use would be exceptional. Digital petitioning of parliament or Downing Street feels tokenistic. Instant online referendums sound suitably dramatic but the practical obstacles to these being workable are significant.

One difficulty is how to open up the political system while maintaining its integrity. The use of the internet has the virtue of speed and simplicity. But there are technical issues – repeat voting, the disenfranchisement of those not online – and bigger constitutional considerations – which mandate holds sway? Ultimately politics is often about trade-offs: each referendum result could reflect the popular will but their cumulative effect may not be satisfactory even to the people who voted in them.

No political party will resolve all these issues in 2015. What matters for now is which political party looks like it best understands them and is willing to think openly about them. Which political party starts from first principles by looking to give people more power and freedom? Without doubt that party is the Liberal Democrats. We will not navigate our way through the new politics with parties that view the journey as undesirable or unnecessary.

The task of re-moulding the state to better enfranchise people is not limited to reform of political institutions. All of the reforms I have discussed put more power in the hands of the individual. That sound principle should be extended more widely.

It is a clear liberal concept that the consumer interest takes precedence over the producer interest. It should be professionally rewarding to work in a hospital, but the institution exists to serve the patients, not the staff. Teachers should be valued and supported, but the main purpose of a school is to advance the achievement of the pupils.

It is this insight that places liberals at the forefront of the next vital stage of individual empowerment and the delivery of public services – personalisation. It is an exciting vision for the future.

The private sector has seen a revolution in the personalisation of services. When new members join a gym they select the exercise classes and routines to match their individual ambitions. Some people will be mainly driven by a desire to lose weight, others by a wish to be physically stronger. Some members will prefer exercising in a social environment, other will enjoy training alone. There is not a one-size-fits-all requirement for new gym members – they custom-make their own fitness regime.

The most imaginative and competitive forces in the private sector have taken personalisation even further. There is no divine decree that makes some supermarkets successful; it is the result of the decision by millions of people to give them their custom. That requires the supermarkets to be hyper-alert to the demands of those customers. Their key insight, which has revolutionised retailing, is that data gathered from loyalty cards can be used to personalise a customer experience.

Previously supermarkets discounted the items that they struggled to sell because the customers did not want to buy them. The new outlook is to discount the items that customers *do* want to buy. And not just all customers, lumped together generically, but each individual customer. The discount vouchers are personalised: reductions on the tea bags, nappies, ready-meals that are the favoured choice of that individual customer.

This is a very powerful concept in service delivery. It is a distinctly liberal concept. It is about more than just allowing each store a little bit of flexibility to respond to differing customer preferences in different parts of the country. It is personalising the service for every customer – millions of them – in every part of the country. It is centred on the individual, not the institution. The starting point is the needs of the service user, not the service supplier.

Some impressive progress has already been made in the public sector with the personalisation of services.

The government's 'Troubled Families' initiative, for example, starts with the assumption that a different, tailor-made solution is necessary in every case. The families often have many problems and come into contact with the state in a variety of different ways. But each family has distinct needs. Some may require a focus on persistent truancy from school, others may need to address specific issues with drug addiction. Some families may have become overwhelmed with looking after disabled children or struggling with accumulated debt.

Personalisation works even better when the tailor-made service is being designed *by* the service user rather than just *for* the service user.

The most established example is for adult social care. During my lifetime, as Britain has become a more liberal country, there have been huge shifts in social attitudes. Previously, people with disabilities were effectively imprisoned in large and unresponsive institutions. They were the ultimate victims of a one-size-fits-all, producer orientated mentality. They were powerless.

Personalisation in its simple form allows people in these circumstances greater freedom to make decisions. That might include living in an institution they prefer or supported living in the community. It might include being able to choose social pastimes that interest them rather than being obliged to participate in activities that bore them.

More advanced personalisation gives the individual responsibility for his or her own care budget. Caring for a person with adult social care needs can cost a considerable amount of money when all the different services are taken into account, and yet the service user has traditionally had no scope to prioritise within this budget. When individuals have the capacity to exercise control over the money spent on them they should have this power.

That in turn allows the service user to diversify into using the services of different service suppliers. There is no reason why the individual cannot use their personalised budget to join an art class run by a community group or a physical activity club run by a self-employed fitness trainer.

Not every recipient of adult social care will feel comfortable with making decisions. But that is not a reason for denying freedom to make decisions to all service users. And those with more limited decision-making capacity may still wish to nominate a personal assistant whom they trust to make decisions on their behalf that are a better reflection of their preferences.

There are more forms of social expenditure that allow for greater personalisation.

Traditionally unemployment offices were very crude in their efforts to find suitable work for people. A generation ago the service consisted of putting the vacancies on a board and putting the unemployed people in front of the board. Insomuch as the service was customised, there was an acknowledgement of the differing skill-sets of people with white-collar and blue-collar employment histories.

But the barriers to returning to work vary enormously from one individual to another. One person may require retraining because their very specific set of skills has become redundant. Another person may have a medical condition which still allows them to work but only with an employer willing to offer flexible working hours. Another person in a rural area may be held back by not having a driving licence.

It makes no sense to *not* customise the service. Keeping a person unemployed for many years is soul-destroying for the individual and expensive for the taxpayer. Empowering that person to dismantle the barriers they face benefits everyone. But the biggest winner is the individual: rather than being pushed into a series of pointless and demeaning activities he or she is able to shape his or her own destiny.

Further pioneering work has been done during this parliament on personalising offender rehabilitation services.

The social consequences and financial cost of reoffending are both unacceptably high. The opportunities for innovative solutions are enormous. One pilot study has sought to put offenders at the centre of their post-prison resettlement plans by involving them in the design of their rehabilitation service. This might involve a greater emphasis in any given specific case on measures to improve the individual's health, social skills or literacy. This tailor-made approach begins in prison and is continued after release.

Those who showed commitment to the project in this pilot study and desisted from offending were able to make applications to a fund to aid their resettlement (paying the deposit for a flat, for example). The goal was to give the prisoner choice and control over his or her own life in return for the prisoner taking responsibility for their rehabilitation.

In many of these areas there need to be safeguards. An individual who displays no inclination to find work but wishes to live indefinitely on benefits should not have that option open to them. The ex-prisoner who re-offends despite being on a rehabilitation programme may need to return to prison as a further punishment.

Power comes with responsibility. Those who do not exercise it responsibly must face the consequences. Indeed, responsibility gives meaning to power. That is true for these personalised services. It is true too for a voter who knows that their vote will have meaning rather than being 'wasted'. It is the miserable alienation caused by the traditional models of power that leaves people disengaged from the consequences of decisions. If a person has no power to build their own path through life they feel no great inclination or obligation to walk down it.

It is necessary to see all of these liberal ideas in the round. The public debate usually concentrates on one area in isolation. The argument is made, for example, that the House of Lords benefits from not being elected, or that councils lack the wherewithal to exercise greater powers, or that personal care budgets are too administratively complicated.

For a Liberal Democrat, however, these ideas are part of a coherent package. What underpins them all is the wish to put more power in the hands of the individual and trust that person to exercise that power. It is a dramatic shift from 'we know best' to 'you know best'.

It is not a shift that non-liberals relish. They fear losing control. They possess an urge to measure their contribution by how successfully they have managed to direct people's behaviour. Their goal is to bend people to fit their will, to put them in a mould. This is the prescriptive management style that has typified British government and public debate.

But it no longer meets the needs of our times. It is out of sync with the liberal age. It chafes against the free spirit of our national character. The era of unthinking conformity has passed.

The opportunity in 2015 is to shape a liberal Britain that pushes these concepts further. A more decentralised, personalised, empowering politics – a more decentralised, personalised and empowered country.

Chapter 5

Sustainability

Britain's long-term success depends on the implementation of policies that last beyond the five-year mandate of a single parliament. It is beholden on each of the parties to set out a vision of how our country can prosper for the benefit of future generations.

We need an economic strategy that enables Britain to generate the wealth needed to raise individual living standards and fund our shared public services. We need a budget strategy that means we live within our means rather than heaping debt on the shoulders of people who have yet to be born. Our reliance on borrowed money has left us living on borrowed time.

So too has our reliance on dirty and diminishing fossil fuels. We must decarbonise our economy to avoid the catastrophic consequences of man-made climate change. Britain led the industrial revolution. The challenge now is to be in the vanguard of the post-industrial revolution, at the cutting edge of the new, clean, green technologies.

And we need to invest in physical infrastructure so our economy can grow and our people can enjoy greater freedom. We need more houses, secure and renewable sources of energy, and a transport system that keeps us, and our businesses, connected, both to each other and to the world.

All of these ambitions are achievable. They require political leadership. They also require a clear sense of ideological direction.

Financially incontinent socialism or stop-the-clock conservatism will not prepare Britain for the challenges of this century. Britain's long-term success depends on the triumph of liberalism.

The Liberal Democrats are the party of free trade, competition, consumer choice and wealth creation.

Economic liberalism is transforming the lives and future prospects of billions of people around the world. Trade and investment are creating new markets, new jobs and new opportunities on a daily basis. Living standards, life expectancy and educational standards are all on the rise. Across the developing world, people are being freed from grinding poverty. Capitalism, far from being in crisis, is unleashing the commercial innovation, scientific exploration and technological invention on which human progress depends.

In Britain our standard of living has been completely transformed by the wealth-generating benefits of the free market. Back in 1970, 85 per cent of households had an indoor toilet; today it is over 99 per cent. Thirty-seven per cent had central heating then; today it is 98 per cent. Far more households have cars (52 per cent to 76 per cent) and washing machines (66 per cent to 96 per cent). These changes have all happened during my lifetime.

This transformation has been funded by the proceeds of successful capitalism. The UK economy was worth £591 billion in 1970 (at today's prices); now it is worth £1,613 billion – an increase, in real terms, of 173 per cent. Most people can now afford items that were considered a luxury a generation ago. The redistribution of this extra wealth has also raised the living standards of people not in work, such as pensioners.

It is not socialism that has driven this progress. Every time that Labour has left government the level of unemployment has been higher than when they came to power. Labour has had two periods in office during my lifetime and on both occasions their legacy has been a state of economic devastation. It is the poorest people that have been most cruelly let down by their failures.

If Labour's ideas were ever going to work, they would have worked by now. Labour has recently had an extended time in national government, winning three consecutive general elections with large majorities. They are the dominant party in most of the poorer parts of the country. So why do those areas remain poor? If socialism was the solution, Labour would have achieved its objectives by now and made itself redundant.

It is assumed that the reason poor areas are represented by socialist politicians is because voters think that socialists are most likely to improve the lives of the poor. In fact, tragically, the opposite is true. Socialism creates and entrenches poverty, both here in Britain and internationally. Despite spending billions of borrowed pounds on welfare and social programmes, the legacy of the last Labour government was higher unemployment, higher welfare bills, and millions of people left dependent on state hand-outs.

Britain's economic progress – occasionally thrown into reverse by socialism – has been powered by economic liberalism. That is what saved Britain from disaster in the late '70s and what will see us emerge stronger from the economic catastrophe of 2008. The task today is to secure the economic recovery now underway, and, crucially, to ensure that everyone benefits from it.

The flagship economic policies of this government have been Liberal Democrat policies. We have not been pulled along in the slipstream of the coalition; we have made the running.

The budget deficit inherited by this government was horrendous. The British economy had shrunk by 7.2 per cent. By 2009, the British government was running an annual deficit of 11.5 per cent of GDP – the highest level in the European Union apart from Greece. In cash terms the annual shortfall was £157 billion – money plundered from future generations to pay the bills for the failures of the present.

No serious or responsible political party could turn a blind eye to our national predicament. I am proud that the Liberal Democrats were prepared to confront it and, over the last five years, have saved our country from economic ruin.

The Conservatives could not have achieved this alone. After supporting Labour's dangerous deregulation of the banking sector and promising to match Labour's spending commitments in the previous parliament, their track record lay in ruins. And after failing to win the 2010 general election, their mandate to take the difficult decisions needed to clear up Labour's mess simply did not exist. Without the Liberal Democrats, we would not be seeing this economic recovery.

Getting a budget deficit under control is not politically easy because institutions and people become accustomed to the benefits of unaffordable levels of spending. Debt-fuelled living feels better than staying within a budget – until the debts get called in. Balancing the books sounds straightforward but it involves facing down huge in-built resistance.

The Liberal Democrats have undertaken this task with clear objectives but a flexible application. Spending reductions have been made across most government departments. Some taxes have increased, some benefit entitlements have decreased, and pay rises, for all but the poorest public sector workers, have been restrained. This has not been pleasant and has made life more difficult for many.

But the alternative was worse. Labour ran up debts in office and then ran away from the consequences in opposition, in what has been a shameful dereliction of responsibility. If we had carried on the way we were going, our country would be bankrupt. Instead, the Liberal Democrats have stuck to the task, flexibly applied but resolutely pursued, and annual borrowing has steadily declined.

The need for deficit reduction will continue in the next parliament whichever party is in government. The judgement in 2015 is which party should be trusted with this vital responsibility.

Labour can be ruled out. Every time they have had an opportunity to show political or moral leadership they have failed. They claimed deficit reduction was a wicked coalition government choice, when in fact it was an urgent necessity. Then they claimed they too would cut borrowing, but have opposed virtually every policy necessary to reduce the deficit. They predicted a rise in unemployment, yet unemployment has fallen. They said growth would be choked off, yet Britain is now the fastest growing economy in the developed world. At every stage, they have put their own political interests before those of the nation and, in so doing, have forfeited the right to be trusted with the management of the economy.

The Conservatives have been partners of the Liberal Democrats in cutting the deficit during this parliament. Most people assumed they would show greater discipline in pursuit of this task than we have. The record suggests otherwise.

The Conservatives like financial constraint in theory but are prone to profligacy in practice. Anyone who thinks that the Conservatives always believe in small government needs to pay closer attention. It has been instructive, for example, to see the strength of Conservative commitment to welfare for the wealthy.

The Conservative deficit reduction plans are also implausibly imbalanced. They are promising to finish the job entirely by cutting spending, while simultaneously promising to protect large areas of expenditure. This would require drastic further reductions in police, local government and defence budgets, all of which have already made substantial savings. Anyone with even a cursory understanding of the public finances can only conclude that the Conservatives do not expect to have to deliver their economic plan in government alone.

It is also doubtful whether the Conservatives can carry the country in the task of completing the balancing of the books. Deficit reduction in this parliament has been controversial but there has been a grudging recognition that it is inevitable and necessary. It has helped that 60 per cent of voters voted for the two governing parties. This has given a greater breadth to the government's mandate. It has also increased the sense of national purpose which both Labour and the Conservatives, as class-based parties serving sectional interests, struggle to capture. Too many people continue to suspect the Conservatives' motives.

The Liberal Democrats have a proven track record on deficit reduction and the credibility to finish the job. Our determination and resolve are beyond question – we understand the necessity of the task.

Britain is not out of the woods yet. We are still borrowing £260 million every day. The annual interest payments on government debt are already £50 billion and are forecast to rise to £70 billion by the end of the next parliament. That is taxpayer money that cannot be spent caring for the elderly or educating the young. It is another sobering reminder that the most vulnerable suffer most when governments lose control of their budgets – the very people whose interests Labour claims to represent.

The competent management of the economy and the elimination of the deficit will be at the forefront of the minds of most voters in 2015. Getting the big judgements right will have a continued effect on our prosperity, levels of employment, interest rates, mortgages and taxes. The Liberal Democrats can look voters in the eye knowing that we have consistently got those big judgements right.

Budgetary discipline is an essential but not sufficient pre-condition for economic success. We also need to build a strong, balanced, sustainable economy capable of generating widely shared prosperity.

The Liberal Democrat economic vision is not based on central planning and state control, but on millions of individuals being economically free to shape their own lives and pursue their own ambitions. We want people to be liberated from both material poverty and from the lumpen conformity of heavily prescriptive government.

Economic success cannot be achieved by government decree, as

Labour still seems to believe. Poverty cannot be ended simply by raising benefit levels. Living standards cannot be improved simply by legislating for higher wages. The cost of living cannot magically be reduced simply by freezing prices.

There are no shortcuts to prosperity. Extra wealth is only achieved by extra productivity. And extra productivity is only achieved by people working harder or more efficiently. That is why the Liberal Democrats are pursuing a twin-track strategy: rewarding work and raising skills.

Our proudest achievement in government has been to cut dramatically the income tax paid by people on ordinary incomes, thereby freeing almost three million low-paid workers from paying income tax altogether. As a result, not only do low-paid workers now pay no tax on their earnings, but twenty-two million others will pay £800 a year less in 2015 than they did in 2010. This was the policy given the highest profile in the last Liberal Democrat manifesto and it has been delivered in full and ahead of schedule. The Conserva tives claimed this could not be done, but they deserve some credit for helping us prove them wrong in government.

By making this our number one priority, the Liberal Democrats have increased the spending power of most British workers, while also decreasing their dependence on the state. Under Labour, people on ordinary incomes were obliged to pay more in tax, and then apply to receive some of it back in benefits and tax credits, making them supplicants of the state. Today they are free to spend or save their own money, earned by their own efforts.

This has also increased the incentive to work. It is often said, and it is true, that prohibitively high marginal tax rates for the highest paid create a disincentive for those employees to go the extra mile by working harder and generating extra prosperity. But that is even more true for people on low and middle incomes. Now the Liberal Democrats have made work more lucrative and therefore more attractive for millions of lower-paid people.

The Liberal Democrats in government have also supported changes to the welfare system which achieve the same objective. Under Labour the system discouraged people from working or working harder by clawing back almost every additional pound someone earned. The introduction of universal credit is putting an end to this outrage: work will always pay, and the more a person works, the more that person will earn.

Getting people off welfare and into work is essential for our national economic well-being. But it also achieves the liberal goal of making people free. A person reliant on the state for their income can never be fully free. Their life is shaped by the conditions imposed on them by the state, their standard of living dependent on the generosity of taxpayers. By contrast, to work is to hold fate in your own hands. Along with the pride that comes from self-reliance is the sense of achievement that comes from promotion and professional advancement. We want everyone to have that opportunity.

That is why, in the next parliament, the Liberal Democrats are committed to making work even more worthwhile by raising the starting point for paying income tax further – to £12,500 – saving people on low and middle incomes an extra £400 a year.

Ultimately, however, the key to increasing people's lifetime earnings and living standards is equipping them with the skills needed to climb the income ladder.

That is why the Liberal Democrats in government have protected the schools budget, focused relentlessly on raising school standards, provided a £2.5 billion 'pupil premium' to boost attainment for low-income pupils, helped to create almost two million workplace apprenticeships, and ensured that more young people than ever before are now going to university.

Our future prosperity demands greater competitiveness. Our competitiveness demands greater productivity. Our productivity demands higher skill levels. And higher skill levels demand that we make a step-change in our educational performance. Deliver that, and we will not only secure Britain's place in the global economy, but will create the conditions for a genuinely liberal society in which everyone can advance as far as their talent and effort can take them.

If Britain is to thrive in the global economy, we not only need everyone to fulfil their potential, we also need every place in the country to fulfil its potential.

London is a global hub city. It attracts wealth and talent to Britain. But increasingly, it also sucks wealth and talent out of the rest of Britain. The solution to London's dominance of our economy is not to pull London down. It is in competition with New York, Tokyo and Shanghai and we need London to be successful. The solution is to raise up the rest of Britain.

Britain's global pre-eminence during the industrial revolution did not originate in London; it began in Liverpool, Manchester, Glasgow and elsewhere. That is the pioneering spirit that Liberal Democrats want Britain's great cities to recapture. We want to see a renaissance in Britain's civic culture with new hubs of wealth-creation across the country.

The mind-set of municipal government has been allowed to lapse into defensiveness. Where once municipal leaders saw their role as promoting economic growth, today many seek instead to mitigate the effects of economic decline; where once they sought to create wealth, today they seek to relieve poverty, usually by lobbying for larger financial allocations from London and Brussels.

That this is the case is as much the fault of central government as it is of local politicians. Decision-making in Britain is too centralised and standardised. With Labour's hard left and 'Militant Tendency' taking control of town halls in the '80s, the Conservatives stripped local government of many of its powers. This had the twin effect of repelling people who, in previous times, might have gone into public service, while suffocating innovation among those who remained. Even the most talented local politicians can feel stifled and disempowered by a workload that primarily entails implementing central government directives and distributing central government grants.

Liberal Democrats believe in freedom. Instead of being diminished and subservient, our great cities should be beacons of innovation and enterprise, not complaining about London but competing with it. The liberal approach is to devolve more power and responsibility to municipal government, in both urban and rural areas. And the cities should look outwards and capture the opportunities of globalisation. Economic twinning arrangements such as those between Liverpool and Shanghai or Nottingham and Ningbo point down a path of future prosperity that need not be routed through London.

Central government can help by not getting in the way but it can also make a constructive contribution. The cities around the world that are thriving are benefitting from infrastructure investment in transport and digital communications. An improved internet service offers economic opportunities in every area, from big urban conurbations to the countryside. And there is no reason why cities in the greatest need of extra private investment cannot offer tax exemptions to attract business.

America provides an interesting model. Rapid economic growth and job creation are happening in areas far from the traditional business hubs of New York and Chicago. Texas is thriving. Seattle, a medium-sized and remote city, has become an Asian-orientated growth point, home to Microsoft, Boeing and Starbucks.

The deindustrialisation of the '80s hollowed out many British cities. Some are starting to grow again, but vast amounts of money have been squandered in the meantime, often on grand cultural projects that were supposed to trigger a wider economic regeneration. The liberal vision for our cities is not of ever more publicly funded galleries and conference centres, designed by exotic London architecture firms, but of a genuine renaissance – driven by the private sector, in partnership with our universities and colleges, with strategic support from municipal government – that will, in ways that cannot be planned or predicted, give each of them a unique economic identity and purpose.

In 2015 voters need to ask themselves which party best understands how Britain can economically prosper in the very different new globalised era. The rigid old class-based politics of Labour and the Conservatives could not be less suited to the task. A vibrant liberalism which cherishes individual creativity is the perfect fit with the requirements of our time.

The Liberal Democrats will take the big economic decisions on which our future success depends: eliminating the deficit; keeping interest rates low; cutting tax; encouraging work; raising skills; supporting regional growth; devolving power and responsibility; and embracing the new opportunities of globalisation.

A characteristic of successful organisations is their ability to think ahead – predicting the challenges and opportunities that will present themselves many years from now. A characteristic of our politics is for forward thinking to stretch only as far as the next election. Yet in 2015 voters will determine not just the shape of the immediate future, but the direction Britain will take for many years to come. Will we stick to a long-term plan to secure Britain's place in the new global economy, or will we turn back, duck those challenges and put instant gratification before long-term reward?

It is a basic human instinct to want to see inter-generational progress. Parents hope their children will have better lives than they have had themselves. Our collective advancement requires the consolidation of previous gains and the ambition to move further forward. This applies to academic understanding, medical research and material prosperity.

A glaring example of where the contract between the generations is fracturing is housing. Previous generations enjoyed a clear link between a good education, a decent job and the ability to live in a suitable home to bring up a family. Now a reasonable home of any kind is beyond the reach of many young and middle-aged people, including professionals whose careers would, in days gone by, have funded the mortgage on an attractive house.

The problem is that housing demand has, for years, outstripped supply. The demand is stoked by a rising population and rising prosperity, a reduction in average household size, the growth of second home ownership and a contraction in the proportion of homes that are available for subsidised rent.

The government can take action at the margins to influence some of these social changes, but not enough to make a fundamental difference. Around 232,000 new households are formed annually; only 107,000 new houses were built in 2012/13.

The social consequences of this shortfall are significant. The opportunities and freedoms that home ownership brought to previous generations are being restricted for millions of people in their twenties, thirties and forties. More people are living with their parents well into adulthood. The average age of a first-time buyer without parental assistance is thirty-seven. People cannot move to take up new employment opportunities. Tenants currently spend about half their disposable income on rent, with this percentage predicted to increase.

If we are to preserve the inter-generational social contract, more new houses will need to be built. The Liberal Democrats support this objective, it is central to our vision for long-term social sustainability.

When deciding where to build additional homes, there should be a presumption in favour of brownfield sites. Many people living in urban areas, far from fearing development, have everything to gain from it. But there will also need to be development on greenfield sites. The future housing needs of our population cannot just be met by building high-density flats in inner-cities. These should be sensitively located, taking into account factors like areas of outstanding natural beauty. Garden cities, within easy reach of growth centres like London, Reading, Oxford and Cambridge, could provide part of the solution.

The Liberal Democrats have championed a 'zero carbon homes' policy in government. The requirement for extra development is a not-to-be-missed opportunity to upgrade our national housing stock. It is much more cost-effective to design solar heating and high-quality insulation into a new building than it is to retrofit it to an old building. The benefit of getting this right is felt in both the long term and the short term: a reduced environmental impact and lower fuel bills.

The new developments should also be socially sustainable. There is a difference between building houses and building a community. It should be possible for residents to buy a pint of milk or a pint of beer without having to get in their cars. New houses should be connected to public transport networks. They should be served by civic amenities that meet people's needs and that foster a sense of belonging. We learnt the hard way, in some of the de-humanising estates built in the post-war years, just how much psychological and behavioural damage can be wrought by poor urban planning.

The decision to address the housing crisis touches on a fault line in British politics. The Conservatives, cautious of change and predisposed towards the interests of the relatively affluent, struggle most to accept the need for significant numbers of new homes. While it is reasonable to be mindful of our heritage, it is worth remembering that all houses were new once. To deny to the young what older generations enjoy is to pull up the ladder of opportunity. A rhetorical commitment to extending life chances rings hollow if it is not translated into action to ensure young people get the chance to live out that most basic of human desires: to be independent of your parents, in a place you can call your own, where you can build a life or raise a family.

An effective transport infrastructure is essential to meet our long-term economic and social ambitions.

A 2013 report by the Civil Engineering Contractors Association found that the United Kingdom's GDP could have been 5 per cent higher, on average, every year between 2000 and 2010 if our infrastructure had matched that of other leading economies. Instead our roads are more congested than those in France and Germany, while our railway network is antiquated and struggling to cope with increased passenger numbers.

Building the infrastructure needed to be a successful modern country requires a long-term approach. Britain is suffering from decades of short-termism and deferred decisions. The south east of England has the same number of airport runways today as it had in the '50s, despite the rapid expansion of air travel. HS1 between London and the Channel Tunnel is the only stretch of high-speed railway built in my lifetime and it is only 67 miles long. The last major motorway development was the M25 in the '80s.

Britain suffers by comparison with other countries in Europe. Amsterdam Schiphol airport has six runways and serves more destinations in the United Kingdom than London Heathrow with its two runways. The speed of trains on the French inter-city network exceeds those of our inter-city trains.

The most dramatic changes are taking place in the fast-developing economies of Asia. In two decades China has built the biggest high-speed train network in the world and an underground system in Shanghai with more stations than the London Tube. Modern airports are dotted across Asia, in Beijing, Shanghai, Hong Kong, Seoul, Delhi and dozens of smaller cities.

Improving our transport infrastructure has social benefits for people in Britain. At peak times our road network is intolerably congested and passengers are crammed into trains like cattle. Relatively short journeys to see friends and family can become daunting endurance tests, with delays commonplace and discomfort almost guaranteed.

The economic benefits are even greater. If people cannot be transported efficiently to work or between meetings, they become less productive. If goods cannot be moved efficiently down the supply chain, the cost to the end consumer rises. If our main airports cannot function efficiently during peak periods or when there is adverse weather, time is lost, trade is disrupted and commercial relationships become strained.

The Liberal Democrats have started the long-haul task of addressing Britain's transport infrastructure deficiencies. London's fast-growing population will be moved more efficiently when Crossrail, the largest infrastructure project in Europe, is completed. Electrification will improve the speed of trains on major routes like London to Bristol and into South Wales. Motorways are being widened at key pinchpoints, and the go-ahead is being given to HS2, which will increase capacity and travel speeds between London and Birmingham, and, in time, Manchester and Leeds.

Our inadequate infrastructure is a damning legacy of decades of short-termism between alternating Labour and Conservative governments. Their failures are in the past – we are now looking to the future.

No area embodies the need for long-term planning better than the environment.

It is important that we define the environmentalism that Liberal Democrats believe in. We want to keep our air clean and our rivers uncontaminated. We want to protect our coastlines from erosion and our low-lying areas from flooding. We value our countryside, our national parks and our areas of outstanding natural beauty. We want to protect the natural environment and our many species of animals and plants. We want to see a reduction in unnecessary waste: less packaging, more recycling. We want to encourage clean forms of transport: cycling, walking and public transport. We want our homes, offices and factories to be less polluting, increasingly powered by clean and unlimited renewable energy sources. And we want, across the economy, to incentivise people and businesses to reduce their carbon emissions to stave off catastrophic climate change and the human suffering it will otherwise cause.

This is a comprehensive package of environmental values. What it is not is a rejection of modern society. Unlike the Green Party, we do not believe that capitalism is inimical to environmentalism; that economic growth is the problem. Instead, we believe that capitalism, that great driver of technological innovation and scientific discovery, can deliver man-made solutions to the problem of man-made climate change. Our objective is not to resist people's legitimate expectations – to own a car or go on a foreign holiday – but to ensure that car manufacturers and airlines are incentivised to provide their products and services in ways that do not destroy the environment.

Getting a sustainable balance is essential to making long-term environmentalism viable. The Liberal Democrats support Britain having sufficient numbers of houses and a functioning transport infrastructure. Our contention is that this is compatible with environmental objectives. We reject the position of those who disregard environmental concerns: they are being irresponsible by putting short-term interests ahead of long-term consequences. But we also reject the argument that we can protect the environment *or* we can improve living standards, but we cannot do both. This is a Luddite false choice and the British people are right not to be convinced by it.

The Liberal Democrats in government have demonstrated how this balance can be achieved. We have transformed, in a short space of time, Britain's environmental profile. Renewables now constitute a higher proportion of Britain's energy. In the last year, onshore wind generation increased by 62 per cent and offshore wind generation by 53 per cent. Solar, wave and tidal clean energy generation altogether rose by 76 per cent.

The Conservatives have become increasingly hostile to these changes, questioning not only the desirability of the policies, but the need for them. Climate scepticism, in the face of considerable scientific evidence, has become fashionable in today's Conservative Party.

If Britain is to become a global leader in the new green economy, turning a potential cost into a significant economic benefit, it will be because of Liberal Democrat leadership. Energy market reform, a big increase in renewable electricity generation, the creation of the world's first Green Investment Bank, the setting of a carbon price floor, a national home energy efficiency programme, support for electric cars, further progress in international climate change negotiations – slowly but surely we are decarbonising the British economy, putting in place the foundations for sustainable green growth.

All of these sustainable policies point in one direction: a successful, liberal future for Britain. More work opportunities, greater prosperity, less debt, more homes, a world-class transport system and a clean environment.

Chapter 6

Globalisation

The great backdrop to our political debate is globalisation. The world order is being transformed as power shifts from the established industrial nations towards the new economic titans, China chief among them. This revolution will have a profound impact on virtually every aspect of our lives.

Every voter will need to decide which political party best understands this revolution and can best equip Britain to respond to it. This is not a sideshow, it is the main event. It needs to inform all of our political thinking.

The phenomenon of globalisation – the integration of national economies through trade, investment and migration, powered by new technology – is an example of applied liberal economic theory. It should be unsurprising, therefore, that liberalism offers the best route-map through this new terrain, and that liberals are best placed to avoid its pitfalls and seize its many opportunities.

A liberal approach begins with a simple state of mind: we should be outward- not inward-looking. We should have the self-confidence to engage with others in the belief that we can succeed and that they can also benefit from our contribution. We should not be fearful of interaction with people from other countries or assume that they wish us ill.

Britain's historical success has been heavily reliant on engaging with the world and taking a global role. We possessed the spirit of adventure and ambition to discover whole new parts of the world. We were instrumental in forming the key international institutions and codifying international law. We did not hide ourselves away, timid and defensive, frightened of the unknown.

Interaction between different people is becoming easier and more common. Tourism, study, business and commerce are bringing us ever closer together. It would be a strange irony for Britain to have held an outward-looking disposition when the outside world was, for most people, either unknown or unreachable, but to retreat into our shell now it has become more accessible and familiar.

In the same vein, we should, in our national mind-set, look forward not back. Every person is torn between the competing instincts to hold on to the familiar or to seek out the new. There is always comfort to be derived from sticking with the tried and tested, clinging to nurse for fear of something worse.

I am certainly not dismissive of the achievements of the past. I can find reassurance and inspiration in the methods of my predecessors. Britain's contribution to the scientific and economic advancement of humanity is dauntingly impressive.

But human progress is reliant on people not being content just to hoard what they already possess. It is only by embarking on new journeys that we discover new frontiers. We can build on the achievements of the past and in turn create new monuments to the visionary instincts of our era. Our predecessors who built the infrastructure and institutions that made Britain the world's leading power were pioneers. They took their ideas and systems to every corner of the globe. We would betray their legacy if we were not to display the same restless spirit.

An outward-looking, forward-thinking, confident Britain has enormous international potential.

Our response to globalisation requires us to deploy the full range of liberal ideas – economic, political, social and personal. They accord with our national strengths and are in tune with the requirements of a globalised economy. We have at our disposal the right template to succeed.

Economic liberalism is transforming the world, raising the living standards of billions of people. Countries that have for centuries been weighed down by poverty are now seized by a new energy. They have embraced free markets and free trade and adopted the spirit of inventive entrepreneurialism. The effect has been to liberate the talents and dynamism of their own people.

Britain's response must be to harness that same energy by continuing to liberate our own people to create new inventions, enterprises and jobs. We can be global leaders, exporting our ideas and products to burgeoning new markets. Our politicians should provide a framework of stability, the rule of law and a sense of mission, but it is by setting free the talents of the British people that our national potential will be fully realised.

Political liberalism requires us to challenge the parts of our system that have become stale, anachronistic or redundant. The best ideas are those that survive exposure to intense scrutiny. So we should question received wisdoms and bland orthodoxies.

Our political model has been subjected to continuous change. Ideas that were once controversial, like the widening of the franchise to women, are now universally accepted. Our parliament was widely admired and imitated around the world. But we have lost momentum and come to rest on our laurels. New democracies do not copy our electoral system for the House of Commons. Even when we recommend a system to others we do not recommend our own. The modern world demands more meaningful choice for the individual citizen than our electoral system provides. The House of Lords, meanwhile, is impossible to justify to anyone with even the most partial understanding of democracy.

Social liberalism is necessary to ensure that every person in Britain realises his or her full potential.

Many countries in the process of rapid development are heavily dependent on the leadership provided by their educated elite. Economic and political power is narrowly held and jealously horded. This is typical of countries in the earlier stage of modernisation.

Britain is in a different phase. We cannot rely on a small cadre of people at the top and, with less than 1 per cent of the world's population, we cannot rely either on weight of numbers. Instead, we must compete through the value we add, the quality we bring, the excellence of our ideas. Our future is as a knowledge economy, powered by brain, not brawn. Yet too many of our young brains are not being properly stretched, too much human potential still goes to waste.

In the past, social liberalism has massively enhanced opportunities for all. Universal education provision allowed the children of poor parents to learn to read and write. Public libraries provided access to knowledge and inspiration for those unable to afford books. Universal healthcare warded off disease through public inoculation programmes and made the prospect of illness or accidents less terrifying for those unable to pay for private treatment.

The next stage of social liberalism can serve our population well again and give Britain a competitive global advantage. The era of big-state controlled solutions has ended. An empowered and discerning public demand more freedom and discretion. The task today is to push power, money, information and choice down to the individual citizen. We need liberalised public services that are more responsive to individual requirements with better collective outcomes for our whole population.

Perhaps most important for Britain, and where we currently have the greatest advantage, is the *personal liberalism* afforded to our people, and how we use that freedom.

The attributes that Britain will need most in the years ahead are innovation, individuality, creativity and originality. It is these qualities that have helped us lead the world in scientific invention, social sciences and the arts. The success of our creative industries is a product of our national disposition and our capacity for unconventional thinking.

Stifling conformity or the dead hand of uniformity are the opposite of what Britain requires. New ideas are not incubated by state command; they bubble up from the minds of free-thinking individuals. The greatest inventors and entrepreneurs were not directed by central planners or government experts – quite the opposite. They challenged orthodoxy, broke from the consensus and called time on the status quo. And their boldness was vindicated.

In Britain both the left and the right suffer from policy prescriptions which fail to understand or capture the essence of what Britain will require to succeed in the era of globalisation.

The international liberal age is best understood by instinctive liberals. Liberal Democrats can intuitively grasp the market forces that drive globalisation and the internationalist politics that shape it. Our values are the values that sit easily with our national attributes and will enable us to succeed. Liberal Democrats do not favour freedom, choice, innovation and creativity because we have made a flip-chart assessment of the virtues that will serve Britain best – these are our core convictions. But they also accord perfectly with the requirements of our time.

Liberal ideas are establishing themselves around the world. In my lifetime more countries – in Eastern Europe and Latin America, for example – have become democracies and free societies. Large countries with closed economies – India, for example – have embraced free markets and opened up to trade. More people are travelling and sharing ideas; university education is internationalised. The internet has had a transformational impact on human interaction. While there is still much progress to be made, it is the nationalists and isolationists who stand on the wrong side of history.

An international liberal age cries out for a liberal response. Yet the Conservatives, Labour, UKIP and the Welsh and Scottish nationalists, in varying ways and to differing degrees, all struggle with the reality of globalisation. It is important to understand why each of these parties is fundamentally unsuited to the task of leading Britain through this dramatic new era.

In contrast to liberal internationalism, the right offers instead a narrow nationalism. While Labour's response to globalisation is to fall back on the state, the Conservative response is to fall back on the nation state. Conservatives feel most comfortable with a detached Britain, sentimental about the past, fearful of the future. Their engagement with the fast-moving world is instinctively cautious and wary. UKIP seeks formal detachment; the Conservatives, more pragmatic, submit to engagement with the wider world, but their prevailing mind-set is one of fearful reluctance rather than ambitious confidence.

Understandably, the Conservatives instinctively venerate the institutions that most obviously embody the nation state. What stirs the Conservative soul is the pomp and pageantry that draws heavily from our past. It does not seem odd to Conservatives to appropriate our national flag for their party-political rallies because, in their minds, the interests of the Conservative Party and the interests of the nation are indistinguishable.

Patriotism is a quality, and one that all politicians should possess. But a politics that genuflects to the nation state and that commits itself to its unaltered preservation is not one that can make sense of our increasingly interconnected world.

The obvious manifestation of this unease is the torturous ongoing Conservative soul-searching about Britain's relationship with the rest of the European Union. Many of their technical objections about the role of the EU Commission or Parliament have some validity, but their anxiety about the European Union is not, fundamentally, about the minor details of the constitution or treaty negotiations. It is felt in their gut. It is the symbolism of the European Union flag and anthem that rile them most.

Conservatives are generally most comfortable with the institutions and groupings that have a foot in the past rather than those that look resolutely to the future. In their dealings with the rest of the world, they prefer continuity to change, and typically look for familiarity rather than opportunity.

Conservatives invariably arrive at international summits eager to demonstrate that they are 'batting for Britain'. They are right to uphold our national interest, but they are mistaken to believe that other countries always want to bowl Britain out. A less defensive posture would allow greater scope for finding mutually beneficial outcomes, but Conservatives struggle to let down their guard. Their principal goal in every meeting is to avoid defeat, not to seize victory. To return home having protected the status quo is the outcome that Conservatives invariably demand of their leader.

UKIP represents these instincts in a more concentrated form. Their founding principle is that no other party, including the Conservatives, is doing enough to protect the nation state. I accept that they are not hostile to foreign people or countries per se, and the nationalist strand of politics is represented in a less palatable form elsewhere in Europe, but it remains the case that if isolationism is the price that needs to be paid to preserve the integrity, even purity, of our institutions and people, then that is a price UKIP make a virtue of being willing to pay.

The Scottish and Welsh nationalists make the same boast, although in their case the nation state would be smaller, and the price they would pay higher still.

Meanwhile, Labour's default instincts – collectivism and state intervention – are the precise opposite of what Britain will need to succeed. We will prosper through the invention and imagination of our people, yet Labour assumes that groupthink is superior to the ideas of the free-thinking individual. It not only rewards conformity, it promotes it. It prefers the single choice of the state to the millions of personal choices made by free people.

Labour looks to a powerful state to create the conditions for human improvement. We are invited to subjugate our private preferences to the needs of society, as defined by 'progressive' politicians. In this misguided world view, it is the politicians who know best; it is they who will make us richer and freer.

While Labour politicians feel at ease with internationalism when it takes the form of cultural diversity and international cooperation, they seem entirely unable to understand or respond to economic globalisation, seeing it only as a driver of inequality and a threat to their traditional blue-collar supporters. Like their trade union paymasters, they view increased competition, greater consumer choice and improved economic efficiency as threats from which the workers of Britain – and Europe – must be protected.

This is what economists know as the 'lump of labour' fallacy, which assumes there are only so many jobs, and so much wealth, to go around. The reality is that the rising living standards of billions of people across the globe are creating vast new markets for Britain to do business with, while simultaneously raising more funds in the poorest countries for social programmes like healthcare, sanitation, education and housing.

Yet the Labour leader, when assessing the impact of globalisation on Asia, is unable to look beyond 'sweatshops'. And as he grapples with how globalisation might impact on Britain, he appears equally pessimistic and fearful, warning of the dangers of being dragged into a 'race to the bottom'. He seems to see no opportunity for shared advancement and mutual benefit. Labour is left with a narrow and nationalistic view of human progress.

Those on the harder left and the Greens represent these instincts in a more concentrated form. Theirs is the politics of protest: the target, the 'forces of capitalism'; the setting, the perimeter fence of an international summit or the headquarters of a multinational company. Their ambition for the future seems to be a rejection of the progress that is incrementally liberating the world's poorest people and its replacement with a romantic agrarianism.

Britain can succeed in an era of increasing economic globalisation but it will not happen by chance. We need to consciously embrace the mind-set, the ideas and the policies that will maximise our national potential. That requires a government with a particular disposition.

So the big decision for every voter in 2015 is whether to support a political party that has a positive view of globalisation or one that is more pessimistic.

Liberal Democrats believe that Britain can benefit from greater interaction and need not be excessively cautious or fearful. We are confident about our national strengths and our contribution to the wider world.

Our opponents are more wary of the outside world, believing either that our sovereignty or our wealth can only be protected by retreating to the margins. They are making a truly massive mistake. All change is discomforting, but hiding from inevitable change does not make it go away. Globalisation is not about to stop. China and India are not about to throw the process of urbanisation and development into reverse and return to their fields.

Most people are naturally unsettled by change. The other parties, to differing degrees, are promising to protect Britain from the changes that are transforming the world. The Liberal Democrats, by contrast, are telling people not what they necessarily want to hear, but what they need to hear. Britain will not prosper over the next generation through isolationism and retreat. That is the route to decline, marginalisation and, eventually, bitter recriminations. Britain will only prosper by being outwardly internationalist.

This is what the Liberal Democrat embrace of internationalism and globalisation means in practice.

First and foremost, it means maintaining an independent and globalised foreign policy. Britain remains a major presence on the global stage and we should use our influence to positive effect.

We are the only country that is a member of the European Union, the United Nations Security Council and the Commonwealth. We are the sixth largest economy in the world with commercial interests that sometimes find us in competition with countries that are otherwise our allies. We are the only G7 country that has achieved the UN target of spending 0.7 per cent of GDP on international development. We have one of the biggest military budgets in the world and a sophisticated diplomatic network. And we have a remarkable degree of soft power which makes Britain a global leader in disciplines as wide as scientific research and fashion.

These assets give Britain huge opportunities to shape the world. That benefits us directly. We want a stable and peaceful political environment, free markets and respect for international law. It also benefits others at the same time. We should aspire to spread the liberal values that have benefitted us. Britain should be a strong voice promoting free speech, democracy and human rights.

The opportunities to spread Britain's benign global influence are increasing, not decreasing. Our most important bilateral relationship is with America and we have vital working relationships with other major Western powers like Germany and France. But now the scope for widening our alliances is growing. Emerging new powers like South Korea and Mexico share many of our instincts and opinions; working closely with them will be mutually beneficial.

The benefits will not just be felt at international summits. Britain needs to be engaged internationally to attract new jobs and investment to our country. The fastest-growing economies are to be found in Asia and Latin America. We need the companies and countries in those continents to look towards Britain. We should aim to be their first port of call. If we cut ourselves off or only engage half-heartedly they will bypass us and call elsewhere.

New bilateral friendships provide opportunities for new forms of cooperation. The threat from global climate change requires a globalised response. Emerging powers like Brazil have an instinctive attachment to environmentalism and a keen willingness to work with partners like Britain. We are forming beneficial partnerships with other countries and global charities to deliver our development goals. Threats to our security are also becoming globalised; the internet and international travel are proliferating and complicating the danger we face from terrorism and organised crime. So working with other security and law enforcement agencies is essential for our protection.

The Liberal Democrats' enthusiastic embrace of internationalism also demands a constructive attitude towards institutional cooperation.

Britain should remain an active member of the European Union. It is the most significant multinational institution in the world. No European power wishes to leave it and many countries harbour an ambition to join it.

The EU gives Britain greater scope for diplomatic force magnification and projection. We are leaders in this area, admired and listened to by our European partners. Our ability to shape global events is enhanced by having the capacity to co-opt other European countries to our agenda.

The EU gives Britain enhanced scale in global affairs. It should not usurp the independent diplomatic policies of its constituent countries, but it can provide critical mass. China can ignore most European countries and marginalise the bigger powers like Britain or France, but it cannot overlook Europe as a whole. We benefit from being in a grouping which makes it harder for others to divide and rule the European countries.

Britain should not participate in monetary union. A major global economy like Britain can maintain its own currency and set its own interest rates. Nor should we submit ourselves to the degree of fiscal integration that will be foisted on eurozone members. Decisions about taxation, spending and borrowing are important features of our democracy. They should not be given away.

Where Britain does benefit hugely, however, is from our membership of the EU single market, the world's biggest. It allows our businesses to export across the Continent. It attracts global investment to Britain from companies seeking a platform within the single market. We need to deepen the single market so that it includes service industries where Britain is traditionally strong.

The EU also badly needs real reform. The mind-set of the EU elite is disdainful of public opinion. The politicians are too detached; financial accountability is disgracefully inadequate; terms and conditions within the bureaucracy are too generous and many spending programmes are too wasteful. Britain should not be satisfied with superficial reform. The ambition to build an 'ever-closer union' should be reversed. 'Britain where possible, Europe where necessary' should be our mantra.

Britain should continue to participate in the G7 and make greater efforts to raise the value of the G20.

The G7 benefits from being a narrow group of broadly like-minded nations, but that is also its weakness. It has no representation from outside the West except Japan. The risk for the G20 is that its breadth of representation leads to lowest-common-denominator decisions. That would be a missed opportunity. We need active forums that allow for enhanced Western cooperation with China in particular, but also, in different ways, with countries as diverse as India or Saudi Arabia.

None of this is more likely to happen if Britain stands back. The G20 can be a forum for meaningful cooperation on the biggest challenges of our time: spreading the economic benefits of globalisation through enhanced free trade agreements; cooperating on new and cleaner sources of energy; combatting extremism and the violence it breeds; helping to protect the internet as a forum for the free exchange of ideas. Progress on these issues is not merely of theoretical benefit to people in Britain; it is central to the well-being of our country in the decades ahead.

Britain should champion an ambitious and reformed United Nations. We should continue to support the UN in its efforts to uphold international law. It should feel uninhibited in its denunciation of human rights abuses. We should not adopt a moral relativism that holds leaders in some countries to a lower standard than we would accept in our own country.

The UN should continue its leadership role in humanitarian and disaster relief work, in education and healthcare, in economic development and in the fight against preventable disease. All of these endeavours benefit mankind and Britain should be a proud supporter of these goals.

The UN Security Council needs to evolve to better represent the changing world order. The current permanent membership is not so dated as to be totally anachronistic but it is showing its age. America, China, Britain, France and Russia should be joined as permanent members by India, Japan, Germany and Brazil, with accommodation also found for African and Middle Eastern representation. With increased status comes enhanced responsibility and the onus must be on all countries with a global role to think beyond their narrow national interest.

Britain should maintain its role in the Commonwealth. It is a unique forum which allows us to engage constructively with a wide variety of different but generally friendly countries.

And Britain should remain as a substantial military power with membership of NATO.

The Cold War that made a global conflict an ever-present danger provided the rationale for the formation of NATO. But the world today carries more diverse and unpredictable security risks. It is highly unlikely that Britain will in future fight a war on its own but we should have the capacity to make a meaningful contribution to international security endeavours. To do otherwise is to abdicate responsibility for defending the values in which we believe. There is an isolationist strand within the Conservative and Labour Parties and it is explicit in the UKIP platform. Liberal Democrats believe it is not good enough to just stand aside when faced with threats to life and liberty. It may not be possible or desirable to intervene on each and every occasion, but we should not make it impossible for Britain to ever contribute by giving up our military capacity and alliances.

An internationalist outlook requires Britain to possess a globalised disposition even in our domestic considerations.

London is indisputably a global hub city. It is a centre for finance, politics, business and the arts. Being a global hub city creates pressures. People want to live, study and work in global hubs. That makes housing, hotels and restaurants more expensive. It puts pressure on transport systems. Those with an inwards disposition are inclined to relieve this pressure by keeping the rest of the world out. Liberals with our outwards disposition believe we must equip London with the infrastructure it needs to remain a global gathering point.

Britain is hugely advantaged by having a global hub city. It pulls investment into our country. It is a magnet for human talent. The goal should not be to diminish the status of London but to spread the benefits. The HS2 railway is the physical manifestation of this ambition. The other great cities of our country should also develop into more powerful cultural, commercial and academic hubs, as many cities in America or Germany have done with such success.

Our universities enjoy a global reputation. Their output is enhanced by opening new campuses in Asia or cooperating with other universities. Our businesses have new chances to explore new markets. And our people can benefit from globalisation. There are exciting opportunities for students to study abroad. There is more scope for people to work abroad, without restriction elsewhere in the EU, and often through inter-company transfers further afield. There is far more foreign travel than a generation ago.

Those with an inwards disposition are unsettled by these changes. The Conservatives and UKIP are nervous about migration and undervalue the benefits that business people, academics and students bring to Britain, or the benefits our own people accrue from living, studying or working abroad. Labour and the Greens are nervous about competition, seeing it as a threat to their uncompetitive 'social model'.

For all of them the primary objective is to mitigate the threats from globalisation, both real and imagined. The Liberal Democrats, by contrast, understand that globalisation's threats are vastly outnumbered by its opportunities, but that we cannot tackle the former or seize the latter unless we are prepared to engage with the outside world and shape it.

Of all the manifestations of globalisation, none generates such strong feelings as immigration – an issue that touches on the most sensitive aspects of national identity.

We need to be mindful of the impact immigration has on public services. A large and sudden influx of immigrants can significantly increase the competition for finite public goods like social housing, school places and hospital beds, and politicians need to ensure that supply increases with demand, and that rationing is, and is seen to be, fair.

We need to ensure that our system of social welfare provision is not open to abuse. Freedom of movement within the EU is based on a right to work, not a right to claim, within the single market. Those who come here to work should do just that. Out of work benefits should not be available to new arrivals on day one and should not be paid indefinitely.

We need to make sure that our border controls function effectively, with a system of entry and exit checks that allow us to count people in and count them back out again so we can identify those who are outstaying their visas and living here illegally.

And we need to ensure that those who come to Britain from other countries make every effort to integrate into British society, defined not by flags and symbols, but by the liberal values on which our laws and customs are based. In practical terms, we need to ensure people are able to speak English and that we do not allow our communities to become unhealthily segregated. Segregation is never desirable or ideal, whether it is imposed, as in apartheid South Africa, or self-imposed, as happens in some towns in Britain.

But none of these issues should blind us to the fact that the benefits of immigration – if properly managed – outweigh the costs. It may not always be popular to say so, but immigration enriches Britain and isolation would make us poorer.

At the top end of the labour market, globalised businesses are increasingly unconstrained by national boundaries. These companies do not automatically belong in, or have fixed obligations towards, any one country. They want to be located in the global hub cities where the brightest and most innovative people congregate. It is a competitive world, and Britain, at the moment, is highly competitive, but that advantage is not automatically granted to us. We need to make sure that we remain a magnet for global talent and investment.

At the bottom end of the labour market, the people with the lowest skills feel under pressure. But in a globalised economy the way to protect people is not to lock out the competition, although it appears to be superficially attractive. Businesses that are more productive and profitable can expand and create new jobs. That is why, even as Britain draws in labour from elsewhere in Europe, we are also witnessing a sharp fall in unemployment. There is not a static quantity of jobs. Indeed, new immigrants, often highly motivated, can create new jobs, some of which will be filled by domestic workers. The task is to ensure that the domestic workers are equipped with the skills needed to fill the jobs.

Many businesses also rely on migrant labour. There are often labour shortages in areas like agriculture or the care sector. Our public services also depend on migrant labour filling both high-skilled jobs like NHS doctors and lower-skilled jobs like cleaners.

And Britain benefits from the wider cultural embrace of globalisation. We should treasure the finest art exhibitions coming to our country. We should be proud that Oxford and Cambridge are universities with a global reach and reputation. We should enjoy the success of the Premier League and the memories of the London 2012 Olympics and Paralympics. Our theatre, television, businesses, media and restaurants are internationally admired. These are all manifestations of globalisation and our willingness to absorb its consequences.

We have choices. Britain could become an inward-looking, fearful country. Or, as a halfway house, we could grudgingly accept globalisation while being reluctant to appreciate its virtues and slow to seize its benefits. Alternatively, Britain can make a success of globalisation and possess a self-confident and outward-looking attitude. This is the Liberal Democrat choice.

Globalisation is the big fact. It is the backdrop to everything. If we make the wrong choice we will find that many of our ambitions for other areas of politics are unsustainable or undeliverable. As we seek to make a virtue of the liberal age, in this area as in all others, the right choice is the Liberal Democrat choice.

Conclusion: A Liberal Party of Government

The Liberal Democrats stand before the country as a party of government.

Our contribution in office has transformed the prospects of Britain. The ruinous budget deficit that imperilled our country has been reduced and will be eliminated in the next parliament. Unemployment is lower and more people are in work today than ever before. Responsible economic policies have kept interest rates low and protected homeowners from repossessions. Britain has more businesses than at any time in our history. The economy is now bigger than it has ever been and growing more strongly than in comparable industrialised nations.

As well as turning around our economy, the Liberal Democrats have started to build a more liberal society. The combination of reduced income tax and universal credit are helping people on low and middle incomes by incentivising and rewarding work. Pensioners have new freedoms to spend their savings and security over the future value of the state pension. Crime has fallen to the lowest level since the independent survey began in 1981, including sharp falls in violent crime. Liberal Democrat ideas like the 'pupil premium' and extra apprenticeships are giving greater opportunities to young people who previously struggled to achieve their full potential.

Britain now looks to the future with greater confidence as we expand our trade with the fast-emerging economies across the globe. The 2012 Olympic and Paralympic Games showcased Britain's organisational competence, creative ingenuity and inclusive instincts. Progressive changes like the equalisation of marriage law have taken our country another step down the road to a more generous and less judgemental society. The communications revolution and the success of our universities are opening up enormous opportunities for today's young people that did not exist for previous generations.

In the decades before 2010 the Liberal Democrats existed on the fringes of politics. We had all the outward manifestations of a political party preparing for power: we published manifestos, held conferences and selected candidates. We were sometimes successful in local elections, but our efforts never amounted at the national level to anything definitive. Through these many bleak years in the wilderness a stoical band of activists kept the fragile flame of liberalism in Britain alive. Government alternated between the Conservatives and Labour. Voting for the Liberal Democrats was a demonstration of faith but not a means for determining the future direction of our country.

The marginalisation of the Liberal Democrats was itself a barrier to the party gaining extra support. Many people assumed that the party would never again be in government. It was claimed, sometimes even by those who were sympathetic to our ambitions, that the Liberal Democrats were a 'wasted vote'. And even those who countenanced the possibility that the Liberal Democrats might govern again doubted whether the party had the necessary fortitude for the task. We were seen as lacking the required mettle to make difficult decisions about the economy or national security. People were willing to vote for the Liberal Democrats in local elections but not national elections. Our leading politicians were derided for their lack of experience of ministerial office.

Now Britain's national political landscape has been transformed.

In 2010 there were widely believed to be two parties of government – Labour and the Conservatives – and the electorate was invited to choose between them. In 2015 the electorate will have a choice between three parties of government. The straitjacket of the old class-based duopoly has been ripped open.

The Liberal Democrat track record in government is deserving of support but the case for the Liberal Democrats in 2015 is forward-looking, not backward-looking. Globalisation is changing the world rapidly and fundamentally. The stale assumptions of the past will not equip us to succeed in the future. Britain will need to possess liberal attributes if we are to maximise our national potential.

We must be outward-thinking, willing to embrace the opportunities of global economic growth. We must be economically liberal, encouraging enterprise, work and wealth creation. We must be politically liberal, giving power and responsibility to people to shape their own future. We must be socially liberal, promoting policies which allow every person to reach his or her potential and contribute to the full. And we must be personally liberal, valuing free expression, individuality and creativity.

This is the liberal age. It would be a tragedy if, at this time, our country did not have a viable liberal party to support. A party that both intuitively understood the liberal age and had the ideas that Britain will need to be successful. But in 2015, in Britain, we do have that party. It is tried and tested in government. It has displayed resolution and imagination. It is uniquely equipped to lead Britain through an exhilarating new liberal era.

It is the Liberal Democrats.

Acknowledgements

I can only do what I do with the professional support of the team working with me – Wendy Pharoah, Val Perigo, Tom Baycock and Bobby Hewitt – and because of the loyalty and indefatigability of the Taunton Deane Liberal Democrat membership.

About the Author

Jeremy Browne has been the Liberal Democrat Member of Parliament for Taunton Deane since 2005. He was a Minister of State in the Foreign and Commonwealth Office from 2010 to 2012, where his specific responsibilities included Pacific Asia and Latin America. From 2012 to 2013 he was a Minister of State in the Home Office. His book prescribing a liberal response to globalisation – *Race Plan* – was published in 2014. Jeremy lives in Taunton and London with his partner Rachel and their daughter Molly.

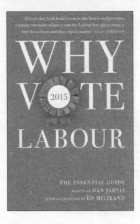

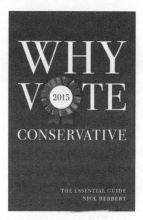

Also available from Biteback Publishing

THE POLITICOS GUIDE TO THE 2015 GENERAL ELECTION

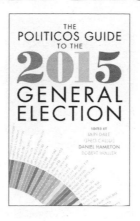

EDITED BY IAIN DALE, GREG CALLUS, DANIEL HAMILTON & ROBERT WALLER

The essential guide to the most eagerly awaited general election in recent history. Here, in one volume, is everything you need to make up your mind in the 2015 general election. This is a unique guide to the state of the parties, policies and issues in the run-up to next May's polling, including expert predictions from political pundits.

With its unique guide to the key marginal constituencies that will make up the battleground, expert commentary and comprehensive opinion poll analysis, this book will arm you with all the facts and figures you need to make an informed choice at the ballot box.

It also features lists of prospective candidates, examples of historical precedent, analysis of the key marginal seats and a comprehensive assessment of the political landscape as the country moves onto an election footing.

464pp paperback, £19.99

Available from all good bookshops
www.bitebackpublishing.com